COSMIC HEALING

A Comparative Study of Channeled Teachings on Healing

ALAN YOUNG

DeVorss & Company, Publishers
P.O. Box 550
Marina del Rey, CA 90294-0550

ISBN: 0–87516–609–1

Library of Congress Catalog Card No.: 88–70721

Cover photo courtesy of
Anglo-Australian Observatory,
N.S.W., Australia.

Printed in the United States of America

Contents

Acknowledgments

Grateful acknowledgment is made to the following for permission to quote from their books and manuscripts:

The Foundation for Inner Peace, P.O. Box 635, Tiburon, CA 94920: *A Course in Miracles* (3 volumes).

L.N. Fowler and Co. Ltd., 1201–1203 High Road, Chadwell Heath, Romford, RM6 4DH, Essex, England: *Divine Healing of Mind and Body*, by Murdo MacDonald-Bayne.

Evarts Loomis, MD, 26126 Fairview Avenue, Hemet, CA 92343: *Lessons for the Aquarian Age*.

DeVorss & Company, P.O. Box 550, Marina del Rey, CA 90294–0550: *The Aquarian Gospel of Jesus the Christ*, by Levi.

Prentice-Hall Inc., Englewood Cliffs, NJ 07632: *The Seth Material; Seth Speaks;* and *The Nature of Personal Reality: A Seth Book*; by Jane Roberts.

Saint Germain Foundation, 1120 Stonehedge Drive, Schaumburg, IL 60194: *Original Unveiled Mysteries* and *The Magic Presence*, by Godfrey Ray King, and *The "I AM" Discourses*, by Saint Germain.

Ruth White, Mary Swainson and The C.W. Daniel Co. Ltd., 1 Church Street, Saffron Walden, CB10 1JP, Essex, England: *The Healing Spectrum*, and *Further Gildas Communications*, by Ruth White and Mary Swainson.

Meredith Lady Young and Stillpoint Publishing Company, P.O. Box 640, Meetinghouse Road, Walpole, NH 03608: *Agartha: A Journey to the Stars*, by Meredith Lady Young.

The White Eagle Publishing Trust, New Lands, Brewells Lane, Liss, GU33 7H9, Hampshire, England: *The Living Word of Saint John* and *Heal Thyself*, by White Eagle, and *Healing by the Spirit*, by Ivan Cooke. (Books obtainable in the USA from DeVorss & Co. or from Church of the White Eagle Lodge, P.O. Box 8182, The Woodlands, TX 77387.)

Psychic Press Ltd., 20 Earlham Street, London, WC2 9LW, England: *Light From Silver Birch*, by Maurice Barbanell.

Introduction

Much has been written about Spiritual and Psychic Healing by individuals residing on this planet. There is, however, a wealth of teaching that has apparently been channeled from the Spirit plane through different mediums during the last fifty years or so. Some of it has been published in book form and some of it has not. I have carefully studied many of these teachings (totalling over 7000 pages) and I have extracted from them the spiritual wisdom that specifically relates to healing.

It seems possible that this information could contain a greater wisdom because of its source and because it would presumably be less affected by the collective consciousness of this planet and the beliefs of humans in physical bodies. However, in reading and researching these numerous books that claim to be channeled from the spirit plane, it became apparent that there were different levels of consciousness or spiritual development on the part of the spirit entities who transmitted the information through the channel.

Some of the teaching seems very profound and illuminating and coming from a source of great wisdom. Other teachings are valuable and full of truth but appear to originate from a slightly lower level of evolvement. Nevertheless, they throw new light on Life and Spirituality and so have been included to the extent that they relate to healing. Some of those which fell into this category have been omitted simply because they contained little if any information involving healing.

Other writings seem to have come from a level of understanding and growth that is similar to or lower than that of many teachers who are still in a physical body, and they therefore lie outside the objectives of this book. In other cases the writings were considered unsuitable because the source or the channel had apparently sought power or glory for themselves.

The teachings selected were then arranged in a fairly uniform manner to make comparison easier. A concluding chapter explores the features that the teachings have in common, thus arriving at what one might call the very essence of Cosmic Healing. *Lessons for the Aquarian Age* describes it this way: "In the New Aquarian Age, Cosmic Healing will be practiced rather than Spiritual Healing which is incomplete. The latter consists of the desire of the healer to heal, merged with the desire of the patient to be healed, whereas Cosmic Healing consists solely of a desire to serve God," and "Cosmic Healing is demonstrated by complete identification with God."

I think it is important that we do not become overly concerned about the actual source of these writings in each case. Whether it is exactly as the human channel or medium suggests, or whether it comes from universal wisdom, or from the medium's own higher self, is not really important if it is the truth. If the reader's intent is to seek the truth and to be open to the truth, then his or her own inner wisdom will advise intuitively on the content, and the reader can let go what does not ring true. Jesus said, "Do not reason with your intellect, for it is limited in its nature and judges from without. The Spirit will reveal all things to you through inspiration."*

**Divine Healing of Mind and Body*, by Murdo Macdonald-Bayne (L.N. Fowler & Co. Ltd., London, England).

I am grateful to the owners of the books and manuscripts from which these extracts have been made for giving me their permission to publish the information in this form. Readers who find it interesting may wish to explore the matter further by reading the complete books.

1

A COURSE IN MIRACLES

THE STORY of how these three volumes (totalling over 1100 pages) came into being is a fascinating and unusual one. From 1965 to 1973 a "Voice" spoke to Dr. Helen Schucman every day that she was willing to listen. She was born Jewish but had no real faith in God or Christianity. Yet it quickly became apparent that the Voice claimed to be that of Jesus. Throughout the seven years of "dictation," Helen resisted the message; nevertheless she felt compelled to continue until the Voice declared that the *Course* was finished.

All that time Dr. William Thetford, her associate in the Department of Medical Psychology at Columbia University School of Physicians and Surgery in New York, faithfully transcribed the information she was receiving, because he was convinced that the teaching had great value. The complete manuscript was first shown to a few people, and then, because of their enthusiasm, photocopies were made and distributed to others. These included Judith Skutch, who eventually was guided to publish the

A COURSE IN MIRACLES is published by The Foundation for Inner Peace, P.O. Box 635, Tiburon, CA 94920.

Course under the auspices of the nonprofit Foundation for Inner Peace. Over 300,000 sets have been sold throughout the world and thousands of lives have been changed.

The *Course* was dictated in the first person, and from the very start of the first book it is clear that the Voice claims to be that of Jesus. He says that the statement "No man cometh unto the Father but by me" does not mean that he is in any way separate or different from us except in time, and that time does not really exist. He says:

> I bridge the distance between God and Man as an elder brother to you on the one hand, and as a Son of God on the other. Awe is proper in the presence of your Creator. Awe is not an appropriate reaction to me because of our inherent equality. Ours is simply the journey back to God who is our home. My strength will never be wanting and if you choose to share it you will do so. I give it willingly and gladly because I need you as much as you need me. I want to share my mind with you because we are of one Mind, and that Mind is ours. The Mind we share is shared by all our brothers, and as we see them truly they will be healed.

Jesus defines the Christ as the Self that we share with him, uniting us with each other and with God. He says, "Christ lives within you in the quiet present, and waits for you to leave the past behind and enter into the world He holds out to you in love."

At least part of the third volume appears to have been dictated by some other teacher who speaks of Jesus as having a special place in healing. It says that he has overcome death because he has accepted Life, and he has recognized himself as God created him, and all living things as part of him. There is now no limit to his power. So in remembering Jesus and calling on his name, we are remembering God and giving thanks for all the gifts God has given us. Jesus has led the way and has remained with us.

The *Course* covers all aspects of spiritual life and growth, but only those parts that relate to healing have been included in this book.

Healing

The *Course* says that sickness is not an accident—it is a defense against the truth. Its purpose is to hide reality. It is a decision, a choice we make. We are told that all sickness is created by our mind which uses the body to manifest what it has created. When sickness appears in the body, it is a sign that the body is manifesting erroneous thought. The body cannot by itself create the symptoms, and to believe that it can is a fundamental error that results in the symptoms. It is a sick mind that thinks the body can be sick. When it can say, "This is not done to me, but I am doing this," it can choose differently, and healing of both mind and body can occur.

God created us as perfect, and we remain that way; all imperfection or sickness is an illusion. The healing power of the thought that we remain as God created us is limitless. It is the truth, and it will release us from all limitations. If we hold to that thought, health cannot change to sickness nor life to death. When we see sickness, pain, or weakness, it is merely a temptation to perceive ourselves as defenseless. If we do not give in to this temptation, we will see the sickness, pain, or weakness—wherever or however it occurs—disappear.

Our minds create pain, which is a sign that we have accepted illusions in place of truth and have denied God. Pain is without purpose and has no power to accomplish anything. Healing is accomplished the instant the sufferer no longer sees any value in pain. If he chooses suffering, he must think it is a small price to pay for something of greater worth, and sickness is chosen. Healing must occur in exact proportion as the valuelessness of sickness is recognized. If we accept the fact that sickness is a decision of the mind for a purpose for which it would use the body, the healing can take place. The mind of the patient is the physician. If the patient were to say, "I have no use for this," he would be healed at once of any form of sickness. All we need do is recognize that sickness is of the mind and has nothing to do with the body.

We are affected only by our thoughts, but we need to remember that we have the power to change them. We have control over our thoughts—no one else does; so there is nothing to fear. We are responsible for what we think because only at that level do we have a choice. Our ability to choose how we think is part of the power of our mind. If we don't believe that we can do this, we have denied the power of our thoughts, and thus we believe them to be powerless. Very few people realize how powerful the mind is, and no one is fully aware of it all the time. It is very powerful and never loses its creative force—it is always creating. There *are* no idle thoughts; they all produce form at some level.

Trying to control the *result* of our thinking will never produce a healing. It is our thoughts that need healing. "The body's suffering is a mask that the mind holds up to hide what really suffers—the mind attacks itself, it is the victim of itself." If we change all thoughts that hurt, we will eliminate loss, pain, and grief; but we need to remember that our thoughts affect others as well as ourselves. "The body is easily brought into alignment with a mind that has learned to look beyond it toward the light." The mind is capable of illumination, but the body cannot learn. Our actions arise out of our thoughts, and that is the level where change is possible and guidance is needed. In that connection, Jesus said that if we are willing to renounce the role of guardian of our thought system and open it to him, he will correct it very gently and lead us back to God.

The source of healing is in our mind because God placed it there: "Deep within you is everything that is perfect, ready to radiate through you and out into the world. It will cure all sorrow and pain and fear because it will heal the mind that thought these things were real." God wants us to be healed, but our minds block the healing. "To heal is the only kind of thinking in this world that resembles the thought of God." We can rely on healing because it is inspired by God and is according to His laws.

We need to create in our minds a clear distinction between the reality that God has created and the illusion that man has created with his mind. All forms of healing rest on this fundamental difference. We are children of God, "a priceless part of His Kingdom, which He created as part of Him. Nothing else exists and only this is real."

Most of us believe that it is the body that must be healed, not the mind. This is because we have given equal reality to Truth and illusion, which is impossible unless the mind were limited to the body, which it is not. This delusion of the mind, therefore, is where the healing is needed and eventually occurs. The body does not need healing. The presence or absence of sickness depends entirely on how the mind perceives the body and wants to use it. "A broken body shows the mind has not been healed—healing shows the mind is healed."

Healing is always certain, but if a patient uses sickness as a way of life, a sudden healing might cause intense depression. The sense of loss can be so deep that he might even try to destroy himself. Therefore, for his protection the healing must wait until he is able to accept it. If we place our future in the hands of God it will release all pain, depression and death. We need to remind ourselves that our life is God's. We do not exist apart from Him.

The *Course* says that the only prayer that is necessary is to repeat God's name. If we repeat the name of God, then little names lose their meaning, temptations disappear, everything falls into right perspective, and we shall recognize the Truth. If we let God's name become our only thought—the only thing that occupies our mind, the only wish we have—then we give an invitation that can never be refused, and God will come and answer it Himself. However, the *Course* also says:

> Prayer is the medium of miracles but the only meaningful prayer is for forgiveness, because those who have been forgiven have everything. Once forgiveness has been accepted, prayer in the usual sense becomes utterly meaningless. The prayer for forgiveness is nothing more than a request that you may be able to recognize what you already have.

Words have no part in healing. The motivating factor is prayer of the heart, not the words used in prayers. God does not understand words; He understands what comes from the heart. Prayer of the heart asks for experiences, not specific things.

The Healer

The *Course* contains many references to our responsibility to heal ourselves and others. It even states that our only function in this world is healing, and that the healing of God's children is all the world is for. Until that becomes our main focus, we shall not know God or ourselves, because we shall use the world in the wrong way and thus experience violence and death.

If we *know* we are one with God and let go all thoughts of sickness, our thoughts can heal all forms of suffering in anyone at any time, for thoughts are timeless. As we deny our separation from God, the world is healed along with us. We have to learn to think *with* God; then we shall think *like* Him and see others as the perfect creations of God they truly are. In this way we fully accept their truth so that they can accept it for themselves. This is healing.

To heal is to make whole and to unite with others who are like us and thus recognize our common Creator. We are given the power to heal our brother* because he is one with us. We are responsible for how he sees himself, and we can change his mind instantly because we are one with him. Recognizing our oneness heals with certainty, cures all sickness, and takes away the guilt that makes sickness possible. We have a holy relationship with all other humans because we are all Sons of God, and this relationship has the power to heal all pain, regardless of its form. When our wills are joined in the oneness, healing takes place.

We are advised to surrender all our abilities to the Holy Spirit because It knows how to use them properly and will use them only for healing. It always seeks to unify and to heal, which is the only way of perceiving the Sonship as One. Healing by the Holy Spirit *always* works; if the healer does not always heal by the Holy Spirit, the results will vary. "All healing is a release from the past, that is why the Holy Spirit is the only Healer. He teaches that the past does not exist."

All of God's children have His total Love and He has given all of His gifts freely and equally to everyone; but unless we acknowledge our complete dependency on God, we cannot know the real power of the Son in his true relationship with the Father. Creation is the manifestation of God's thoughts, which are limitless and infinite in number, and "God's thoughts are given all the power that their own Creator has."

The Holy Spirit teaches one lesson and applies it to all individuals and situations, namely that *all power is ours*. Our vigilance will enable us to use it always and in all ways. It was created to be shared. "The power set in you in whom the Holy Spirit's goal has been established is so far beyond your little conception of the infinite that you

*Sister is also implied by this term, and masculine-gender pronouns are similarly used in this manuscript for convenience' sake.

have no idea how great the strength that goes with you. And you can use *this* in perfect safety. Yet for all its might, so great it reaches past the stars and to the universe that lies beyond them, your little faithlessness can make it useless."

Those who are healed become the instruments of healing. We are never healed alone. But the *Course* reminds us that "the message is first intended for the messenger, and when it has been accepted it can be passed on." In order to heal, it is essential for the healer to allow all his own mistakes to be corrected, and God will show him how to do this if He is asked. In the *Course* Jesus suggests that where there is a need for healing, the healer should think of it this way:

> I am here only to be truly helpful. . . . I am here to represent Him who sent me. . . . I do not have to worry about what to say or what to do, because He who sent me will direct me. . . . I am content to be wherever He wishes, knowing He goes there with me. . . . I will be healed as I let Him teach me to heal.

> Those who have been forgiven must devote themselves first to healing because, having received the idea of healing, they must give it to hold it. The unhealed healer wants gratitude from his brothers but he is not grateful to them. That is because he thinks he is giving something to them, and is not receiving something equally desirable in return. His own ingratitude is a lesson in sickness. Healing is the one ability everyone can develop; and must develop if he is to be healed, yet there is nothing in the healer that others don't have. If he thinks there is he doesn't understand God.

A healer is perfectly safe as long as he is completely unconcerned about his own readiness, but maintains a consistent trust in Jesus' readiness. His sole responsibility is to accept for himself the Atonement, which is defined as occurring when an interlocking chain of forgiveness is completed; we accept God's forgiveness by extending it to others.

Faith is the opposite of fear, and a very real part of love. To have faith is to heal and a sign that we want to share the oneness that we have accepted for ourself.

> Faith acknowledges everyone as a Son of your most loving Father, loved by Him like you, and therefore loved by you as yourself. It is His love that joins you, and for His love you would keep no one separate from you. You see the Christ in him, and he is healed because you look on what makes faith forever justified in everyone.

We must first accept the gift of healing for ourselves and then we can give it to others.

If we remain concerned about the result of a healing, we will limit the healing. It is a lack of trust. We are urged not to doubt that when we have tried to be a channel for healing we have succeeded, even if the symptoms continue to appear. Continued concern appears to be a demonstration of love, yet love without trust is impossible, and doubt and trust cannot coexist. Self-doubt is always underneath the doubt about the result. Maybe there is a fear of vulnerability or failure and shame, or a guilty embarrassment stemming from false humility. It is always some form of concern with the self, not the patient.

We are told to make people happy and they will be healed. If we are happy, we will be healed. If we attempt to heal without being wholly joyous ourselves, we may deprive others of the joy of responding wholeheartedly.

> The only possible whole state is that of love—there is no difference between love and joy, therefore the only possible whole state is the wholly joyous. Healing is a thought by which two minds perceive their oneness and become glad.

> Healing does not come directly from God who knows His creation is perfectly whole. Yet healing is still of God because it proceeds from His Voice and from His laws. . . . When you heal you are remembering the laws of God and forgetting the laws of the ego.

We are told that every situation is an opportunity for healing. We first offer faith to the other, then give him to the Holy Spirit and release him from any demand of our ego. Thus we and the Holy Spirit will see him free and the latter will heal him through us. Joining with the Holy Spirit in a united purpose makes that purpose whole, and it heals. If the healer has faith, he has accepted the Unity of All for himself and wants to share it. We need to recognize the worth of other people and acknowledge their power to create as well as ours. We are all co-creators with God. If we deny the creative power of others, we deny our own and the creative power of God who created all of us.

Forgiveness

Analyzing the *Course* for its teachings in regard to healing, it quickly becomes clear that much importance is placed upon forgiveness. It might almost be considered the key element in healing. We are told that when we forgive, we call upon the strength of Christ within us, and this takes away all fear, guilt, and pain, and ends all suffering and loss.

> Forgiveness is the key to happiness.
> Forgiveness is the only road that leads out of disaster, past all suffering and finally away from death.
> We can find peace only by complete forgiveness.
> Forgiveness is the source of healing.
> Forgiveness is the release from all illusion.

> Forgiveness is the only function meaningful in time.
> Forgiveness is the only purpose of the world.

On the other hand, if we fail to forgive, we create all sorts of problems. In fact, "All problems are caused by unforgiveness." Whenever we suffer, if we look deep enough we will find some unforgiving thought. When we do not forgive another, we judge him or her, and our mind is full of fear, leaving us no room for love and no release from pain. Holding a grievance against someone creates a shield of hate between us and the truth, and we forget that we were made in Love's image. If we don't forgive, we shall judge the other as justification for our failure to forgive. In fact, the *Course* specifically says that it is concerned only with Atonement and the correction of the perception that we are separate from God and separate from each other, and that "the means of Atonement is forgiveness." In other words, if we do not forgive others and ask forgiveness for ourselves, we build barriers that create the illusion that we are separate, whereas in reality we are not.

Some people feel that it is wrong to be asked to forgive. They have been hurt, so they have a right to be angry and ought not to be asked to let it go; forgiving the other would be foolish. This is a natural attitude if we believe that the offense is real instead of an illusion. We cannot really forgive if we hang on to this belief. Forgiveness and hurt cannot exist together—one denies the other. No one who has truly forgiven can suffer or remain ill; real forgiveness brings healing to both. We are asked to see that forgiveness is a natural reaction to distress that rests on error. If we regard it as an unwarranted gift, we uphold the guilt that we want to forgive.

We are to remember that the one who hurt us was also created by God and is therefore perfect. In fact, we are all parts of the Eternal Whole, so in truth there is nothing to forgive. We are always to remember to include ourselves in that forgiveness. Forgiveness is not complete unless we also receive it for ourself, and then our secret guilt disappears. This is our responsibility, otherwise we cannot help or heal another: "Only forgiveness offers miracles." Forgiveness benefits both the one who forgives and the one who is forgiven, for "giving is receiving" and "you accept forgiveness when you forgive."

God has never condemned us and therefore He has no need to forgive us, but His Love is the basis of forgiveness. So rather than ask God to forgive us, we are told to ask Him to teach us how to forgive others. Our willingness to forgive is a gift to God, and His Holy Spirit will extend it forever, making it a potent force for peace and a source of healing for everyone.

If we forgive everyone and everything, then all we look upon speaks of God to us. We can see no evil and there is nothing in the world to fear. And, as we love others, so we love ourselves; nor do we condemn ourselves or others for so-called mistakes. Our only desire is to heal and bless, and as this is what God wills, so healing and blessing take place.

We need to hold the thought that God is in everything and therefore we are to look on everything with love, appreciation and open-mindedness. Separation is an illusion —we cannot be separated from God or each other in Truth. A sense of separation from God is the only lack we really need to correct.

> How does one overcome illusions? Not by force or anger or by opposing them in any way. Merely by letting reason tell you that they contradict reality. They go against what must be true.

When we forgive other people, we release ourselves from these illusions, but if we do not forgive, we bind ourselves to them. If we had no illusions we would have no fear; but truth will correct all illusions. Everything we *think* that we see has been created by fear.

Love

The *Course* also places much emphasis on the importance of Love, which is another key element in healing.

Love is the heart of God—there is no other Love. It cannot change, nor can it be withheld from anyone. It cannot judge; it looks on all as one. Love is a law without an opposite. There is no Love but God's, and what He is, is everything there is. Love created us. Love is what we are; this is our identity. God loves us all equally, and we are sustained by His Love, which will protect us in all circumstances. The answer to all our problems is to put all our faith in the Love of God within us—eternal, changeless and forever unfailing. This Love within us will enable us to resolve all seeming difficulties without effort.

We cannot understand how much God loves us, for there is no parallel in our experience of the world that would help us understand it. There is nothing on earth with which it can compare. There is no other love that can satisfy us, because there is no other love. It is complete, and so it asks for nothing in return. It is wholly pure and gives everyone everything.

Gratitude is an aspect of this Love. Not gratitude that we have more than others or suffer less than others. If it is sincere, it must be joined to Love. We are urged to be grateful for every living thing and thank God that we are not separate from any one of them. It does not matter if others are ungrateful for our gifts to them. If we are grateful for the privilege of giving, our gifts are accepted by the Heart of God Himself. We need not fear Love, for it alone can heal all sorrows and gently waken us from our dream of pain. This is God's final judgment: "You are still my holy Son, forever innocent, forever loving and forever loved, as limitless as your Creator, and completely changeless and forever pure."

We need to let go of all fear. There is really nothing to fear, but we are afraid because we trust in our own strength rather than trusting in God. We tend to associate fear with love because we believe that love can bring pain, whereas actually fear is the absence of love. We are even afraid to give because we fear it will involve a loss for us, which is impossible because God's supply is limitless.

If we will only remember, and constantly reaffirm to ourselves, that "I am as God created me," then fear would have no meaning and would be unreal; and misery and death would not exist. "Fear is a stranger to the ways of love. They cannot coexist." If we fear God Himself, as some people do, then we create gods out of fear and vengeance. If we just feel the Love of God within us, all fear will be eliminated, and a world of hatred would be inconceivable. We are asked to free those who believe they are bound, helpless, and afraid. When we allow love to flow through us, the love replaces their fears.

All love is implicit in creation; all fear is implicit in miscreation. We cannot master our fears by willpower, only by love. "Actually fear is really nothing and love is everything."

The reason we fear love is that it would remove the dark cloud that separates us from God; we would have to "answer His call and leap into Heaven." However, our intense and burning love of God and His for us are much stronger than our ego will ever be. We must include everyone within our love or we will create a place in our mind where the Holy Spirit is not welcome, and this will exclude us from Its healing power. If we do not offer total love, we will not be healed completely. We cannot enter into a real relationship with anyone unless we love all and equally. We can love only as God loves, for there is no love apart from His. Love increases as it is given.

Causes of Disease

Cause and effect are one; we cannot separate them although we try to do so. Healing occurs when cause and effect are brought together. Healing of a disease without the cause merely shifts the symptoms to some other disease. Sickness is anger taken out upon the body, but the body has no feeling, so it does not suffer. It does what we want it to do, but it does not choose and does not judge the road our mind chooses.

The body will naturally stay healthy if we do not abuse it by expecting it to perform beyond its capability or to fulfill purposes for which it was not designed. This could be by overwork, or by ignoring the need for rest and relaxation, or by imposing an excessive strain on muscles or bones, or by ingesting harmful substances.

Pain is a sign that God is denied. It is only our thoughts that cause us pain. Nothing in the world has the power to make us ill. If we seek pleasures through our body without an integration of mental and spiritual awareness, we shall also find pain. The pain is not punishment; it is the inevitable result of thinking that we are our body—and this is the invitation to pain.

Most of us live under a heavy burden of guilt, but the *Course* says that we are guiltless and that God does not want us to be bound by that burden. If we are in need of healing, it indicates that we have denied this guiltlessness. Only if we exchange guilt for innocence can we experience freedom from pain. We can be mistaken, we can deceive ourselves, we can even turn the power of our mind against ourselves, but as Sons of God we cannot sin, because this would violate reality. The Holy Spirit will never teach us that we are sinful. It will correct errors, but this does not create fear in us. Every miracle is "a gentle winning over from the appeal of guilt to the appeal of Love."

The *Course* repeatedly emphasizes that the cause of all sickness and pain, and in fact the cause of all other problems in the world, is a belief that we are separate from other beings and separate from God; and if we will accept the fact that we and every aspect of creation are all part of God, and One with Him, then healing of mind and body and life will be experienced. When we are sick, we have lost touch with the Unity that gives us life; but when we see the truth of that Unity, healing occurs and demonstrates that sickness is not real.

Death

Physical birth is not a beginning, it is a continuing. Everything has already been born. Death is not an ending, because we share God's Life, and the opposite of God does not exist. Death, as mankind conceives it, is only a thought, but it may take many forms, e.g. sadness, fear, anxiety, or anger. The thought seems very powerful and inevitable.

Jesus says that he raised the dead by knowing that Life is an eternal attribute of everything that the living God created. He teaches that there is no order of difficulty in miracles. Miracles are natural because they are expressions of Love, and with Love nothing is impossible. Life has no opposite, for it is God. Life and death seem to be opposite because we have decided that death ends life. If we forgive the world, we will understand that everything that God created cannot have an end, and nothing that He did not create is real.

> Death is the symbol of the fear of God. His love is blotted out in the idea. It cannot coexist with God. Death denies Life, but if there is reality in life, death is denied.

Reincarnation

Reincarnation is mentioned only once in the *Course*, which says:

> In the ultimate sense, reincarnation is impossible. There is no past or future and the idea of birth with a body has no meaning, either once or many times. If it is used to strengthen the recognition of the eternal nature of life, it is helpful indeed.

If it is used to offer preoccupation or pride in the past, or to induce inertia in the present, then it is folly.

The idea of reincarnation is not regarded as essential to the *Course*, so it takes no definite stand on the concept. It does, however, state that if a healer does believe in reincarnation, he should not renounce the belief unless his Inner Teacher advises him to do so.

Live in the Present

The *Course* discusses the importance of living and thinking only in the present and letting go of the unreality of time. It says that *now* is the closest concept of eternity that we can have in this world: "It is in the reality of 'now,' without past or future, that the beginning of the appreciation of eternity lies." If we remember the past as we look on other people, we will be unable to perceive the reality which is now. We are advised to learn to look on everyone with no reference to the past, either theirs or ours, and thus to learn from the present.

Healing cannot be accomplished in the past but only in the present, and this also takes care of the future. Healing is within the present because its continuity is real. "In it are all things that are eternal, and they are one." We need to learn that past pain is an illusion so as not to experience a future of illusions and be unable to release the present.

2

DIVINE HEALING OF MIND AND BODY

IN THE SPRING of 1948 a series of 14 weekly talks was given in England before several thousand people by Murdo MacDonald-Bayne. As the talks progressed, it quickly became apparent that Jesus had taken over MacDonald-Bayne's body and voice and was speaking to the audience through him. Later MacDonald-Bayne described his experience as follows:

> For several months prior to the giving of these talks I would awaken from my sleep at night hearing a voice apparently speaking in me. I could hear the voice and reason what it said at the same time. After many of these experiences the voice said that special talks would be given and were to begin on a certain night when those attending were all chosen. The talks must be recorded so nothing would be lost.

DIVINE HEALING OF MIND AND BODY, by Murdo MacDonald-Bayne, is published by L.N. Fowler & Co. Ltd., 1201–1203 High Road, Chadwell Heath, Romford, RM6 4DH, Essex, England.

> When the night arrived I took my place in the auditorium. Then I felt as if 1000 volts of electricity were passing through me. I did not lose consciousness although I became aware of a magnificent power, a consciousness far above my own. Then I could hear my voice yet it was different, speaking with great authority, an authority of one who absolutely knew. The language was perfect without a flaw, without a hesitation.

All those who were present testified to the wonderful experience of hearing the Master Jesus. For example, one of them said:

> This was a unique and unforgettable experience. No one who heard the talks could ever be the same again. The veritable presence of the Master became so strong a reality to us that it has never faded but grown in intensity and vividness. No description could ever convey the tremendous force of the Presence of the Master, and, through him, the Love of the Father—a distinct evidence more real than anything physical around us.
>
> As the lecturer entered, he was the kindly, smiling man we all knew so well. After a pause of silence suddenly an amazing change took place: a short sharp intake of breath and the very Master was present in the same body but utterly different. He now appeared unusually tall, much taller than the lecturer himself, commanding of aspect, austere and of great authority with brilliant eyes and assurance of power. In dawning comprehension we listened to truths greater than any we had ever heard, and yet we realized they were the same statements we had heard and read since infancy, but only now did we understand their meaning. A love shone through his presence, embracing all of us impartially, universally.

The talks are devoted to a message of Love and Peace and spiritual growth, and they contain a wealth of wisdom for all aspects of our lives. However, in keeping with the theme of this book, an effort has been made to extract only those parts that specifically relate to healing. After studying these the reader may well feel drawn to obtain the full series of lectures to be found in the book footnoted at the beginning of this chapter. The quoted texts are Jesus' own words in the lectures.

Healing

> Christ is the Spirit of God manifesting in the flesh, and has been given all power in heaven and on earth through Love. The Christ of God is the living Presence of God in each and every one of us—the Father manifesting Himself. It is the same in you and in me.

The Christ is within us and nothing from without is of any use to us. We cannot see the Christ because of our ignorance and sin; we can only see Him through the Love of God. When we recognize the Truth that the same Christ lives in us as lives in Jesus, we will manifest the Christ, for we have also been given dominion over all things. If we believe in Jesus, we shall do even greater things than he did.

> Christ, the Son of God, in the heart of humanity reaches out to man urging him to awaken to his Divine Consciousness, for the Christ in each and every one is alive forever. Christ is God and God is Christ. The Christ of God worketh in you 'now.' Live in the realization of this truth so that the truth shall manifest in your life.

No matter who we are, or what we are, we are told to remember that the Christ dwells in us. If we will awaken to the Christ within, the still quiet voice that is all-power will manifest itself through us. This awakening is the realization of our oneness with all, with God who is All. We cannot comprehend the greatness of the Christ in us, for the Christ is ever unfolding the Presence of God that dwells in the soul of man. "The Christ is the mediator between God and mankind; he understands God and understands man. It is the *individualization* of the Spirit of God in manifestation." According to our realization, the Christ manifests in us, and thus we consecrate our lives to God.

If we say in our hearts in love and understanding, "Thy will be done in me," then the Christ will move in us, for Christ is God manifested in the flesh. By recognizing and realizing this Truth, a tremendous force arises within us. If we let the mortal senses be silent, the Christ in us will take possession of our mortal body and be our guide; but when the mortal senses are active, the Christ in us is silent.

Christ is creative energy constantly active from within, renewing every particle of our bodies. The Christ sees and understands falsity and truth and corrects the error. When the error is corrected, the condition disappears. We are assured that we have nothing to fear no matter what illness or difficult circumstances we may experience, because the Christ overcomes all. This is our power, the power of God existing in us. All things were created in the Mind of God and nothing is apart from Him. Therefore in Reality, all is perfect.

Jesus says that he will open the doors so that the great River of Infinite Life will flow out and flood all nations. There is perpetual healing wherever this River flows. So we are invited to open up to It, and let It flow through us to all creatures. We can expand our capacity to receive Life by clearing our mind of limitations. Our beliefs have become a hindrance to the unfoldment of the unlimited. Only if we free our minds from the limitation of ideas and beliefs of others can we receive the unlimited.

There is a great deal of the Christ force imprisoned within our minds, unable to express itself because of our rigid beliefs. As we become more aware of the Eternal Life expressing Itself, It will become more real to us. The brain, the nervous system, and the flesh of the body will become filled with It. Our consciousness is the means through which Life manifests Itself in the body. If we become conscious of God's power, this will renew our body and mind, and bring peace and Love into our heart.

Jesus cautioned us that there must be silence in the outer when the Christ of God speaks from the inner. When we turn our thoughts and our hearts inward, our soul begins to feel the warmth of the Christ of God. What we look upon with our inner vision we will bring forth into our individual life. Only within ourselves can we find the answer. The real sacred place is within ourselves, within our own heart; there we can speak with God. In our heart comes the healing and the Love of God. When we seek within, we will find the Father. If we know this is true, and know ourselves to *Be*, He will manifest through us. When we look without, we see only effects.

Another important factor in healing ourselves or others is prayer. Jesus says,

> Prayer is the sense of the Presence of God and this should be a conscious reality at all times. Real prayer is deep earnestness; it has great attractive power, and I want to impress upon your mind the importance of being earnest in prayer, not to an outside God but communion with the Father through the Christ of God within. When you pray to your Father in Heaven, you must enter into Heaven by closing the doors of the senses that lead to the outer. For only in the heart of hearts when there is the Golden Silence of Love can your prayers be truly heard.

We must worship in Love if we would attain a consciousness of God.

When we pray, if we believe that we have received that which we have asked for, then we will have it. When we ask, we should ask in the Mind of God; it is then established in the Spirit, and what is established in the Spirit must come forth in form, provided we make ourselves receptive to it through understanding Faith. No earnest prayer is ever disregarded. God knows what we are in need of before we ask. God is Love, and we must reverence Him with our hearts full of love. When we pray earnestly in the quiet of our own soul, the whole Universe is brought into action to create and express the answer to our prayer.

We need to give some part of the day to silent growth, thus bringing poise and balance into our whole being. Jesus says,

> Prayer to me was and is the breathing of the breath of life. It is the most powerful thing in all planes and in all worlds. The power of prayer lies in the fact that the prayer and the answer are one. Live in the thought of Love towards all, and your life will become one continuous prayer.

The Healer

> The great mistake most make is to think that I and my disciples have sojourned to some far off place. There is no place, only a state of consciousness; and we are with you now. The more you realize this, the more we can come into your lives and help you. The beneficent law is ever operating in your lives and you have power to help others, only bring them into the light of your own consciousness, raised to the consciousness of the Christ. The great works of healing can be done only when the mortal senses have ceased to be and the consciousness turned towards the Kingdom of Heaven within. My Father has given me power to overcome all conditions, and this power is manifested in you also. Therefore do not look upon others as separate from yourselves and from me, but feel with me in the whole of humanity.

We are urged to let go all strain or doubt and to see the victory of the Christ accomplished in those we wish to help; then it will be established. There are many accounts of healings in the New Testament. These healings were brought about by the same means—the recognition and the realization that the Power has dominion over all things, the flesh having no say in the matter. When we speak from the Christ in the strength of our calm assurance, the false condition will completely disappear. God is omnipresent, and we can bring the troubled Spirit in touch with God instantly.

> The desire to help must come from the heart. In your heart you will find there a Presence that will come forth and will express Itself in you and through you, and your desire will be fulfilled. . . . In helping others, it is far better to show them how to help themselves through the Creative Power of the Christ that dwells within them. . . . This is the great truth that you must hand to every soul—the great gift of God.

In everything we undertake, we need to hold the thought that God never fails, that it is the Father who is doing the work. If we do this then everything becomes possible for us. All our thoughts of Love and Healing sent out without any special direction are of value, and they help everyone. Jesus found from his own experience that the physical body changed through his conscious awareness of the Divine Essence of Love. This power creates all things and attracts everything to it. People are puzzled by the healings that took place 2000 years ago, but Jesus says that there is very little difference in the healings that take place among us today. The only difference is the person who is used, but it is the same Christ that heals. We can understand now that Jesus' thoughts become the healing power that changes disease and death into Health and Life. He says that our work is to cooperate with the Christ so that we may be avenues for healing in all manner of ways.

Healers are constantly to hold the thought that all of the universe is one complete whole, expressing the divine nature of Love. We all dwell in God, and there is absolutely nothing outside of God. We are not a portion of Spirit, but we are one with the whole. Spirit cannot be separated from Itself. There cannot be one particle of substance that is not of God; for it is God alone that is expressing Himself. We need to understand that the great truth of the Omnipresence, the Omnipotence, and the Omniscience of God is complete.

Underneath it all there is only the one Life, flowing from the one Source, the one Spirit manifesting itself in all. If we, who are living beings upon earth, were separate from God, then God could not be Infinite. Anything that separates us from one another is a falsehood; separation denies the Christ in us. "God's consciousness is manifesting in every one of His creations, and every one of His creations exists in His consciousness."

We are because God is. There is no separation because there is nothing outside of God; in fact, God is All There Is. Nor is there any division in God, and we and Jesus and all others with us are one great, united, unlimited whole—one family in which there is no separation, only Love. To be consciously aware of our oneness with God is the open door to freedom. We can be just as much of God as we are prepared to manifest.

Jesus says that if we will listen to his words, we will understand the inner Voice so that our Life will be full, and our bodies perfectly whole. We shall be safe from harm or accident, for the veil that divides us from the Spirit world is very thin. We can pierce it with our thoughts, and thus those on the spirit plane can come to us. When we stand in the Kingdom of God within, no matter what storms are raging in the outer, we are safe in the Kingdom, for in It all power is given to us. We reveal the perfection of the Father through the realization of His Divine Love, which remains always a protection for ourselves and others.

Forgiveness

It is clear from the lectures that Jesus considers forgiveness a very important factor in the healing process. He says:

> Your Father in Heaven forgives you in His heart the moment you ask for forgiveness. It must be the same with you. He has already forgiven your faults when you forgive others their faults. But if you do not forgive in your own heart there can be no forgiveness. In the heart is the meeting place of God and man; you can meet Him face to face when you have forgiven all. Ask for forgiveness, not as a servant would, but as a child would ask of its parent, knowing well that forgiveness was already given by the heart that loves it.

Jesus urges us to be kind to one another and tenderhearted, forgiving of one another; for as God forgives us, so are we to forgive others. Eventually everyone will forgive one another, for only through forgiveness and love can we enter into the joy of Heaven. Jesus' awareness of God is never clouded by injustice; his awareness and understanding of the Father's love enables him to enter into that true state where he could say, "Father, forgive them, for they know not what they do."

> That which is untrue in the outer shall pass away, because from the heart of love comes the healing of forgiveness.

Love

In these talks Jesus puts much emphasis on the importance and power of Love. He says:

> God is Love and Love is God. Love is the center of the whole universe, and from this center a continuous flow of Love flows through every soul and through everything that lives. Love is the affinity in

> minerals; the essence in flowers; Love is expressed in the animal nature. In man Love is expressed in affection, and, when fully realized, the whole being is filled with It and every cell in the body becomes vitalized. There is no other power in the world but Love—it is the Omnipresence of God. You are the creation of the Infinite Life which is Love.

This Love, this mighty power is within all of us. It grows from within us and is ready to be used by all regardless of intellect or education. We have been prepared for It and It will flow through our souls. When we are conscious of this we are conscious that the Kingdom of God is indeed within us. Love is complete in itself, nothing can withstand it and nothing is ever wrong where it exists, and since Love is God, there is no greater power.

> Every creation was created with the fundamental principle of Love harmonizing every action, bringing into manifestation God's Divine nature. Love is the union between God and mankind. So mankind becomes the vehicle for the expression of Love, and this is the true science of living.

Jesus says that when he was incarnated he knew that God was Love, and to be His son he had to be Love also. He found there could be nothing else for him but Love, and no matter what was done to him he still knew that he must remain the Son of God, the eternal ever-present perfect Love that knew no past or future, no sin or death. Even now the Love of God is pouring through him continuously, and as he receives it, he expresses it naturally. That is why the greatest thing we can do is to love one another as he loves us:

> Love dwells in every living soul. Love much and I shall do my work through you. To understand the love of God, you must begin to love more, and as you love more so I shall work in you, and through

> you, because I am love, the Son of the Father of Love. I love all in the world.

We can always receive this wonderful gift of Love that is being poured out eternally. We can experience It for ourselves by opening ourselves up to It. We will not receive it from the external, but It is eagerly waiting to express Itself from the very center of our being. Our mortal sense blinds us to the truth because we look without instead of looking within.

"Love is the Christ, the manifesting power in the world, the power that sustains the whole of humanity." Individually it works for us when we recognize it as the whole. As we become aware of the wholeness of this power within us, we feel it, we know it, we become Love Itself.

The positions we hold in the world mean nothing. What is most important is our capacity to receive and give Divine Love, the true expression of God Himself. When we resent injustice, or our minds are in a state of turmoil, full of envy, jealousy, anxiety, or resentment, there is no Love; Love is the only power in the world that dissolves all these things. In order to know the Father of Love, we must think of Him often; then our hearts will be where our treasure is. We know the Love of God by adoring Him who is Love. And how do we adore that which is Love? By reaching up to the highest that is within ourselves, by giving out the love that is flowing to us from Him who created us, and by becoming aware of this outflowing river of Life and Love that streams through our souls. "To love all is to love God."

If we love with all our heart, soul, mind, and strength, Jesus promises that he will reign in us, and nothing will be impossible to us. The Love of the Father in Jesus is expressed in us. In that Love there is Intelligence, Power, and Wisdom to accomplish all things. The Spiritual body is perfect substance, and every part of our material body will act in obedience to the Christ, the only *Reality*.

Causes of Disease

Many of us seem to lack vitality. Jesus says this is because we live an unequal existence in the three planes of manifestation: Spiritual, Mental, and Physical; or Spirit, Soul, and Body. This unequal state of existence is brought about by our belief in the fact that Life is derived from some external source. The majority of us pay too much attention to the body and too little attention to the Source of Life. It is our mortal senses that deprive us of the power that exists within us. A belief in the outer, a belief in the power of something that has no power in itself is the cause of our weakness.

Love eliminates fear and removes all that is contrary to our true nature. Fear has the effect of changing the chemistry of the body, but these conditions can be overcome by applying the antidote of Love, which is the only permanent power in the Universe. Every thought, movement, or action effects a chemical change in our body, frequently making it inharmonious. But Love is harmony and healing for soul and body. When we let go of our fears we will find that the normal harmonious state of our body will return.

We are told to put away from us all bitterness and anger against another. Nor are we to seek revenge. For if we hold that thought about anyone in our heart, that is what we will create in ourselves.

> Most people in the world have developed through ignorance and have not developed perfectly all round; and this has been the cause of much sickness in the world. Man is hurt by man again and again, and not until man is crucified through his own folly will he open his eyes to the great "Oneness" of all through the Christ of God. There is no power that can harm you against your own will.

Death

We believe in death and decay; but in Reality there is no such thing, there is only change, and this is Life. "How could there be anything dead in the living Universe? How could there be anything dead in the Eternal Living God?" There is change taking place everywhere, but there is nothing dead in that change; every particle is a living particle which changes from one form to another. What ignorant man sees is death; what enlightened man sees is the action of Life. Every particle, even in its process of change, is a living expression of Life:

> There is no death, there is no interruption in the individual life by the advent of death. Death is but a change that takes place where the Spirit sown in the earthly body goes forth in the Spiritual body. It is the Christ that lives now in your earthly state, it is the Christ that lives forever.

Jesus warns us not to cling too tightly to the earthly life, for it is only a preparatory step in the growth of the Christ within. Many are holding too strongly to life on this earth and the things that exist in it. We may use these things wisely, but we ought not to cling to them, nor allow them to cling to us. We have nothing to fear because we lose nothing that is real. No love is ever lost. Most people fear the experience called death, but when we pass through the experience we will find ourselves to be a living, breathing soul, more alive than ever before, for it is the soul that breathes, not the body. We will be overwhelmed by the freedom from limitations that we will experience, while all our false beliefs will drop away. We will be the same living soul, no matter in what way we die. Flesh and blood do not enter into the higher realms, but we will realize that we are the same ones who lived in physical bodies.

Life is not interrupted by the event called death; there is no break in life, in birth or in death, and there is no birth and no death in life. Neither is there separation between those who have left the body and those who are still in the body. We are indestructible spiritual beings and if we accept this truth it will alter our whole mental attitude towards sickness and death. We think we have lost our own loved ones who have died. Jesus assures us that this is not true; they are greater now than they have ever been and they are nearer to us now than they have ever been. Many of our loved ones who dwelt with us on earth have entered into the larger sphere of Life's consciousness and are with us now. Little do we know how close they are. They watch and pray with us.

Live in the Present

"Love" is the eternal ever-present and glorious Life now, which is joy and satisfaction too full to make us look backwards or forwards. We should never be troubled about tomorrow because "now" is the only time. If we make NOW our only reality, then tomorrow will take care of itself. Consciousness can only create now, not tomorrow, nor yesterday. We can only create in the Mind of God moment by moment, and that is now. Our true nature is Divine; we need to let this nature become ours now, because now is Eternity, every moment of Life is now. Therefore we should forget the past, and not worry about the future; the future will be taken care of by our living now.

When we begin to know that all time is the present, we cease to long for things to come in the future, and a great strain drops from us. Peace will come into our souls, and things that troubled us before will no longer bother us. Spirit is all power and directs all things, but if we go within and open ourselves to receive, we can experience the harmony and peace now, and there will never be any other time. Each of us makes the future by our thoughts and actions in the present, and "now" is always the present. We need to make the most of our time in the "now," for now is eternity.

Suffering

Jesus warns us that suffering on the path is inevitable. He says:

> Peace and calm will come into your hearts when you know that you are passing through all stages of the Christ from the birth to the Ascension. The crucifixion means that everyone is crucified. All must pass through their own gates of Gethsemane; some pass through it one way, some another. Thus you are purified through your experience. Do not rebel against conditions but learn your lessons from them. Every experience will render you more power; learn that the beauty of the morning sun comes after the darkness of the night. Do not think that the Father has left you when you find yourself in distress. He is making you more perfect, a more perfect instrument through which He can manifest His Creative Power.

Knowledge is born of suffering until man attains to the consciousness of God. When we reach the conscious awareness of the only one Real and existing Power expressed in ourselves, we will realize that suffering has been the means of the unfoldment of the awareness, and then suffering ceases. The darkness that surrounds us unfolds the Christ in us. When a seed is planted in the darkness of the earth, the Life in the seed unites with the Life in the earth waiting to reproduce it; it grows out of the darkness to express itself in the image and likeness of the seed sown. So does the Spirit of God; the Christ is the seed that is within us and grows out of the darkness that surrounds us. The beauty of the Christ manifests in us as the image and likeness of God. We must not be discouraged if immediate results are not forthcoming. Work is being done in accordance with our thought. This law is infallible.

> Your mind is the mirror of your soul, and even in your suffering you will grow stronger, knowing

> that you are always in the presence of the Father. Darkness is but the absence of light. When your hearts are full of Love there can be no darkness in the soul, for Love is the Light of the world. Truth is the search for the Light of the world. "Love" is the first Cause and when you find this truth you have found everything.

Jesus says that if we suffer, we are to suffer in peace, and he will reign in our life, for God will work within us, and cannot fail; then our suffering will not have been in vain. We shall feel the power of the Christ, and our sufferings will be no more.

3

LESSONS FOR THE AQUARIAN AGE

THE FOLLOWING TEACHING is taken from an unpublished 575-page manuscript that was channeled through a medium, Olive Haisley, for the benefit of Mrs. Amy Loomis about twenty-five years ago. Mrs. Loomis has since passed on but her son, Evarts Loomis, MD, has kindly given permission to include in this chapter what appears to be the essence of this teaching as it relates to healing.

The Preface to this teaching says:

> This manuscript consists of a series of lessons received from Jesus of Nazareth by one whose dedication and selfless service earned the high privilege of this contact and personal instruction. The lessons have been the instrument for her own spiritual illumination and attainment.

Healing

In the New Aquarian Age, Cosmic Healing will be practiced rather than Spiritual Healing, which is incomplete. The latter consists of the desire of the healer to heal, merged with the desire of the patient to be healed, whereas Cosmic Healing consists solely of a desire to serve God. It is more powerful and reaches beyond the spiritual range. It permeates the being of the subject. Cosmic power is generated by emitting vibrations of peace, which are initiated by disassociating oneself from the desire to serve God. If we identify individuals and conditions with God as the Whole, we shall demonstrate Cosmic Healing. If we think of God and the individual as separate, we shall dissipate the power.

Cosmic power is generated within the superconscious mind in this way: if the conscious mind expresses spiritual thoughts, or it desires to serve God, the subconscious mind eventually becomes saturated with spiritual energy. The superconscious mind will then be filled from the overflow of spiritual energy generated in the subconscious mind and will generate cosmic energy in direct proportion to the amount it receives.

To "Be still and know that I am God" remains the key to the development of cosmic power as healing power within the consciousness of both the healer and the healee. The perfection of God is to be incorporated into Cosmic Healing; beyond perfection there is nothing to seek for oneself or another. Perfection reigns supreme wherever God is permitted to control expression.

Cosmic Healing occurs when the so-called healer disassociates the sick one from his consciousness and replaces this one with an all-consuming awareness of God as the Whole or Perfection. It is futile for a sufferer to seek comfort by physical means without a consciousness of God as All.

Jesus says:

> The endocrine glands are to be thought of as the soul of the anatomy. Endocrine function is so clearly related to spiritual expression that as cosmic energy is generated the function of the glands is normalized. The function of these glands is comparable to the soul as operating independently from

> the body and is the index to the co-ordination between the spiritual and physical attributes. Normally their balance is correct, but as one system is developed out of proportion to the other the balance is disturbed and the result is illness, depression, mental disturbance or even insanity.

If we recognize this imbalance between the physical and the spiritual, and recognize God as the Whole, including the sufferer and the would-be healer, cosmic power will be invoked and balance restored. Cosmic Healing is demonstrated by complete identification with God through fusion or union of the physical and the spiritual attributes, and this can be achieved by merely thinking the word *fusion*, feeling the sense of peace flooding throughout the body, and sensing the downward flow of cosmic power.

> Fusion can also be experienced by mentally superimposing the spiritual attribute upon the physical, thinking of the spiritual on the left side of the brain and the physical on the right, about temple level, and drawing them to the center in sharp focus.

This will usually leave one with a conscious feeling of Oneness.

The physical body is subjected to much spiritual force during the process of healing, so sometimes there is a pause or recess from the constant breaking down and replacement of cells.

The Healer

The fundamentals of Cosmic Healing are Peace, Service, Surrender, Disassociation, and Abandonment. The healer is urged to desire above all else a consciousness of Peace within his heart. The peace that passes all understanding can be found there, and we are told that "The vibrations emitted from a mind at peace are powerful beyond human conception."

The healer is also consciously to desire to serve God and literally to walk into His Presence, relinquishing all concerns. Peace will pour in and overflow in a never-ending supply as long as the desire to serve God endures. Service to God by service to humanity is a blessing and a privilege, not a burden. It is to be rendered in love and never as a duty; the latter thought would prevent the attainment of cosmic consciousness. Service to another is actually service to God because the other is in truth His Substance. Each effort to serve accumulates experience until Cosmic Healing is demonstrated.

The purer the desire to serve God according to His will, and without any conscious desire to choose the nature of one's service, the clearer will the revelation come as to the manner of service God desires. The objective is to become a channel to be used as God wills. Service to God generates cosmic power, which is God's power, and a feeling of blending one's own consciousness with that of God's, and this brings a sense of Wholeness. "To serve God is the ultimate goal of existence, but to be eager to attain the goal is to lengthen the distance between you and the goal."

The next requirement is to surrender one's self and every aspect of human experience—physical, mental, and spiritual—and every desire, until one becomes a conscious part of God and literally feels like a cell in the very heart of God, which is our true identity. As such a cell we are complete. Our will is all that we possess in our own right and is the one thing that God requires us to return to Him. Everything else pertaining to our life on this earth belongs to God. Physical life on the earth plane is a school in which the lesson of surrendering our will to God must be learned above all other lessons. Then we shall see that loving God with all our heart, soul, and mind, and our neighbor as ourself, has become the purpose of existence.

We are also to surrender unto God all personal, material, or spiritual concerns until there is not even a subconscious desire to see the fulfillment of that for which we pray. This in itself will energize anyone we include in the thought of surrender. We must even surrender the desire to heal or the desire to serve God. Complete surrender to God is the key to cosmic consciousness and cosmic power. There is only one Source of power in the universe and that is God, All There Is. If we dissociate ourselves from all desire, even the desire to serve God, we become an empty vessel or channel to be filled or used as God wills.

The lessons advise us to go beyond surrender and to completely abandon ourselves to God, then imperfection will be transmuted into perfection, leaving only consciousness of God, during which state cosmic power will flow freely to the one in need and healing will be initiated. Responsibility, credit or recognition for the result are also to be abandoned to God with no sense of personal desire to be included in the act. We cannot serve our fellow men unless we first let go all personal desires and take up the cross which is symbolic of the love we bear for our fellow men. Love heals and penetrates the cells of the body and renders them impervious to attack by bacteria.

The lessons also instruct the would-be healer:

1. to will the love of God to flow through themselves, thinking the word LOVE and feeling the love as it flows. This breaks down the resistance to the power.

2. to will the power of God to flow through themselves to the sufferer, thinking the word POWER. As this is done, the healer becomes one with that power, which then energizes the sufferer's physical body and awakens them to the spiritual beauty of life within the heart. The less the healer dwells upon the recipient of the love and power, the more effective will be the flow.

3. to become conscious of the presence of God, who completely fills all space, and adore Him. To include the one they desire to help, feel a sense of great beauty, and become an open vessel completely filled with the Love and the Light condensing into peace. As this is done, a continuous flow of cosmic energy will be created and flow through the healer's body.

4. to surrender everything to God and simultaneously eliminate every other conscious thought. Also to identify the one to be helped as a component of God, a particle of His substance.

5. to expect a complete healing regardless of the disease, seeing only the beauty of perfection which is God. To accept the healing and give thanks for it. The healing will be measured by the degree of faith.

Preparation before healing is important because cosmic energy requires a more substantial and stable channel than does spiritual energy. We are told to desire to function selflessly as God wills, not as a channel for healing. Nothing is ever beyond the reach of prayer voiced or expressed as thought from an unselfish being. There are no limitations to the power of God, and prayer is the means to fulfillment of our desire to make contact with God. We are not to visualize the condition or the sufferer as we pray, but to see only perfection, peace and cosmic radiance, believing that the healing is occurring and giving thanks simultaneously. We are urged to will the Love and the Light which is the power of God to flow through us to the one in need, and as we do this we shall become one with the power and the other person. If we try to persuade those that we wish to help that God is actually All There Is, and if they will trust Him, He is always able and willing to heal the suffering they so needlessly endure.

Thought is the most powerful of all vibrations generated by human entities either in the physical or in the spiritual form of existence. There is no need to form or utter the words inspired by the thought. If we think of God we bring all good into alignment with a need. We become what we think, so we need to control our thoughts. Thought is the key that turns on the power or places an individual within the radiance of God. The purer the thought, the higher the vibration.

We are to release all conscious effort to serve. The time, the place and the nature of the service will be provided:

> Contacts with those in need are not accidental, but are preordained through the guidance and direction of unseen forces or entities who follow the activities of individuals on earth assigned to their protection or guidance.

It is a mistake to desire to serve humanity rather than God, or to emphasize individual needs, and thus dissipate the power. Opportunities to serve God will be presented—there is no need to seek those needing help. We serve when the need becomes apparent. One of the pitfalls on the path is the desire to impress others with one's spiritual development. Praise from anyone other than God is unnecessary and undesirable. Surrendering one's ego is the supreme test of devotion to God.

We are not required to carry the burdens of others, although at times the temptation to do so is great. The afflicted person is always willing to surrender their burden, but if the healer assumes it, the journey to union with God is delayed for both. The former must eventually resume carrying the load until he has overcome the difficulty which created the problem in the first place. Both are advised to surrender all to God, and to follow their own path.

Cosmic power generated by the desire to serve God will protect the healer from depletion of his physical energy beyond his capacity. Physical fatigue is a signal. It indicates the need for rejuvenation by recognizing God as the whole. We are not reservoirs with a limited amount of resources; we are channels of unlimited Divine power.

Jesus

The lessons purport to be dictated by Jesus, and he states that he has a part in Cosmic Healing. We are to include him in our efforts to serve God by becoming a channel for healing, because he desires to reinforce those efforts. We can become aware of him as an actual Presence, taking the place of any individual we wish to help, and so merging our consciousness with Jesus' consciousness that nothing else remains. We can accept his presence as a constant companion and always a part of our being, as long as we desire to serve God. As we practice this, we shall become confident of our awareness of God as All There Is.

As we believe Jesus is capable of healing disease, so we shall become able to believe that we can heal with Jesus as a cohort. Thinking upon God with Jesus as a constituent of God generates cosmic power, and if this is coupled with the thought of healing, it will channel cosmic power. Prayer in the name of Jesus releases cosmic power. Jesus says that when he prayed for Lazarus and surrendered him unto God, he saw only God where the body of Lazarus lay, thus imaging only the life of God, and this attracted life to the apparently lifeless body of Lazarus.

Jesus also says:

> God desires and needs faithful servants, or healers, who are capable of emitting cosmic energy as they think and breathe, thus igniting the cosmic spark within all who cross their path. Whosoever believes, to him is given the power to heal. You are like an electrode conveying cosmic energy from God or the Source, to any being whom you identify through thought with God. I am ever with the ones who identify themselves with Me in their surrender unto God.

Death

If we let go of the physical body as a natural course of events it will not only render transition to the spiritual level less painful, but actually it will be a beautiful experience. While cosmic power can heal all physical disease, there is a time when the physical vehicle is not permitted to continue. After an individual has completed the transition, we are advised to will the love and the light to flow through ourself and the other person and to do so in the name of Jesus. We are not to grieve for them, but consciously to identify them with God. There actually is no separation between the so-called living and those who have made the transition we call death.

Reincarnation

Though a sense of guilt seems to require us to perform good deeds to pay karmic debt, nevertheless if we desire in our hearts to serve God through service to our fellow men, the debt will be removed, and we can go on our way rejoicing, knowing in our hearts that Jesus has paid our so-called karmic debt.

Suffering and Pain

Physical suffering is a test of faith in the power of God to heal, and the condition causing the pain will be healed as the sufferer surrenders doubt and fear. While the desire to serve God is within the consciousness of an individual, disease is an avenue of cleansing. Pain and frustration are avenues through which spiritual progress is accomplished. To attempt to find a way of escape rather than to continue onward through the obstruction should not be considered. Each obstacle encountered is necessary. As the physical body is caused to suffer or require attention, it is vulnerable to the awakening of spirituality.

Possession

There are millions of entities on the astral plane seeking a physical vehicle which can be invaded and thus become subjected to the will of the invading entity. The possessed person is not capable of functioning normally. An individual who has selfish desires is vulnerable to invasion by entities eager to repeat physical experiences. We can avoid this if we are selfless in our desire to serve God. While a desire to serve God exists in the conscious mind of an individual it is not possible for an entity to invade or gain possession of the body or mind of that person.

Exorcism is not difficult, nor does it require greater advancement on the part of the channel through which cosmic power is directed. The first requirement is disassociation of self, as in any case of healing. Then the invading entity and the one possessed should both be identified with God. Thus we acknowledge God as All Perfection leaving no space within perfection for the imperfection that is evident in the presence of a possession. To merge with God all that belongs to God is the true technique.

We are warned that there is no justification for the practice of letting the mind vacate the body while attempting to heal and not remaining conscious of all things and people surrounding us.

4

THE AQUARIAN GOSPEL OF JESUS THE CHRIST

THE FOLLOWING WORDS are quoted from the Introduction to *The Aquarian Gospel*:

> Levi was born in 1844. . . . [and was] a close student of the religions of the world from childhood. . . . He entered into the deeper studies of etheric vibration, determined to solve the great mysteries of the heavens for himself. Forty years he spent in study and silent meditation, and then he found himself in that stage of spiritual consciousness that permitted him to enter the domain of these superfine ethers and become familiar with their mysteries. He then learned that . . . every thought of every living thing is there recorded. . . .

These records are known as the Akashic Records.

THE AQUARIAN GOSPEL OF JESUS THE CHRIST, transcribed from the Akashic Records by Levi in 1906, is published by DeVorss & Company, P.O. Box 550, Marina del Rey, CA 90294–0550.

> When the mind of man is in exact accord with the Universal Mind man enters into a conscious recognition of these Akashic impressions, and may collect them and translate them into any language of earth with which he is familiar. . . . Every person has his own distinct vibration and when the reader [of the Akashic Records] fully understands the law of discrimination his whole being is tuned for the reception of the one particular tone and rhythm, and it is impossible for any other tone or rhythm to make the slightest impression upon him. . . . It required many years for Levi to learn the Law of Differentiation, and to come in rapport with the tones and rhythms of Jesus of Nazareth. . . .

Thus *The Aquarian Gospel* is a record of the life of Jesus taken from these Akashic Records, which is more complete than the New Testament. For example, it covers the life of Jesus between the ages of 12 and 30, years which were completely omitted from the New Testament. Also it is possibly more accurate as it has not been interpreted by the Church and the translators over the centuries.

The source for this chapter is therefore an exception to that stated in the Introduction, since although the words were recorded in this century by a medium, they were spoken in the first century. However, it seemed to be appropriate to include *The Aquarian Gospel* as it contains much helpful information on the subject of healing, which is hardly surprising in view of the thousands of healings performed by Jesus. It is also interesting to compare the actual teachings of Jesus at that time with the teachings that are purported to have been channeled from him by others in this century as reported in the first three chapters.

All those who approach the reading of *The Aquarian Gospel* with prayer and honest intention to know only the Truth can judge for themselves whether or not there is truth in these words. There is, of course, a great deal more spiritual wisdom contained in the whole book in addition to the following selections which especially relate to healing and Jesus' teaching on this subject.

An interesting cross-reference was found in the unpublished *Lessons for the Aquarian Age*, which are purported to have been given by Jesus in recent years (see ch. 3), in which Jesus says, "*The Aquarian Gospel* not only explains the hitherto unrecorded portion of the life I experienced apart from the one I knew as My family, but expresses the Truth that God actually is All There Is."

Healing

Jesus used various methods for healing. Sometimes he laid his hands on people and they were healed. Other times he just said "the Word" and they were healed. He told some individuals to go and wash in certain pools, and others he anointed with a holy oil (ch. 74, v.3). One time a child fell in a pool and drowned, and Jesus lay upon the lifeless child and breathed into its mouth. Then he called out loud for the soul to return. The child revived and lived (74:17–18). Sometimes Jesus was not even in the presence of the sick person. For example, a nobleman whose son was sick came to Jesus and asked him to come to his town to save his son. Jesus did not go; he just stood in silent prayer for a few moments and then said, "Your faith has proved a healing balm; your son is well" (86:2–5).

Another time he used a psychological approach. A child asked Jesus for help because her father was a drunkard and used all the money her mother earned to buy liquor, so the mother and children were always hungry. Jesus went with the child to her home, found the drunkard, and said:

> My brother, man, made in the image of our Father-God, will you arise and come with me? Your neighbors are in sore distress; they have lost all they had

in a fierce fire, and men must build their homes again and you and I must lead the way.

The man got up and went with Jesus and saw the damage and the misery. Jesus asked the man to lead the way in reconstruction, saying that other men of Bethany would help him. The man went to work and the homes were built again. Then he saw his own poor dwelling and his heart was moved to make it into a real home. He worked as he had never worked before and everybody helped; soon the hovel became a comfortable place filled with love. The mother and the children were delighted and the father never drank again. "A man was saved and no one ever said a word about neglect or drunkenness, or urged him to reform" (92:13–28).

When he was asked why he used different ways to heal, Jesus said that disease is a discord in the physical body, and discord can be produced in many ways. Sometimes the individual is too relaxed and then disharmony results. Sometimes he is too tense, and then another form of discord occurs. Disease has many forms and there are many ways to heal (75:5–8).

Healing did not tire Jesus. He often healed and taught all day, and then far into the night without even stopping to eat (105:9). His friends tried to force him to rest but he said that while he was working to help the needy he found rest in the arms of God whose angels brought him the bread of life (105:13–14).

Jesus frequently stated that healing depended on people's faith. One time he was with a crowd of sick people at the edge of a healing spring. The people believed that at a certain time of year their god came down and gave power to the water of the spring, and that the sick who then plunged into the water and washed would be healed. They were standing around waiting for this to happen, but Jesus asked them why their god blessed the spring one day and then the next day took his blessing away? If their god had power, it could fill the waters full of healing ability every day. He said that the healing power of the water of that spring was not a special gift of God but the healing power was faith. So, he who believed with all his heart that he would be healed by washing in the spring would be made whole when he had washed; and he could do this at any time.

Then many people rushed into the water and were healed, but Jesus saw a little child who was too weak to move and no one helped her. Jesus asked her why she waited, and the child replied "I need not haste; the blessings of my Father in the sky are measured not in tiny cups; they never fail. . . . When these, whose faith is weak . . . have all been cured, these waters will be just as powerful for me." Then Jesus said, "Behold a master soul! She came to earth to teach men the power of faith. . . . The waters of the fount are love; the potency is faith, and he who plunges deep into the living springs, in living faith, may wash away his guilt and be made whole. . . . " (41:21–24).

Jesus said that all men are sons of God, and if we live a holy life we shall always see and understand the works of God, and in His sacred name we shall be able to perform these works (91:35–36). However, while all men can gain the power to do these things, they must first conquer all the passions of the lower self; and they can do this if they want to (91:40). Whatever tends to purity in thought and word and deed will cleanse the human body (68:16). And with such purity come Power, Light, and Christ Consciousness (71:9).

When man understands the fact that he is a son of God, and that within him lie all the powers of God, then he will be a master mind and will be able to control all the elements (92:11). After his resurrection Jesus said, "All my life was one great drama for the sons of men. . . . I lived to show the possibilities of man. What I have done all men can do, and what I am all men shall be" (178:45–46).

The Healer

One time the disciples tried to heal an epileptic child but failed to do so. They then asked Jesus why they could not heal the child. Jesus told them that their great success in all their former work had made them careless, and they had forgotten to recognize the power of God and forgotten to pray. "There is no faith without the prayer of faith. Faith is the wings of prayer; but wings alone fly not." Prayer and faith can move mountains; however, their failure may have been a blessing because the greatest lessons that we learn in life come from our failures (130:16–21). On the other hand, Jesus warned them that when a healing does occur, they should not rejoice because they had been instrumental in the healing; the power and the glory belong to God (140:11).

One day the disciples asked Jesus to tell them who was allowed to heal the sick and cast out demons from those who were obsessed. They also reported that they had stopped another man from healing because he was not one of them. Jesus replied:

> Do you imagine that you own the powers of God? And do you think that all the world must wait for you to do the works of God? God is not man that he should have a special care for any man, and give him special gifts (131:31–38).

In all the world there is only one energy, but it comes in many forms of power, all of which are of God (96:3–7).

Jesus said that when God calls on us to serve He will always supply our needs. If our efforts to serve are not appreciated, we are not to react with negative thoughts, because if we do, it will dissipate the power (122:17–18).

There is much emphasis throughout *The Aquarian Gospel* on the importance of service. For example, Jesus said that if we honor man, we in fact honor God, and if we help another, we will serve God. So, if we want to serve

God, we may serve friends, relatives, and strangers and even those who want to hurt us. We may also assist the poor and help the weak (26:11–14). If we give our lives in sacrificial service to the All of life, God will be pleased (28:25).

On another occasion Jesus said that a perfect life is one that is spent in service for other humans, and for animals and birds (37:19); also, that the most efficient prayer that we can offer to God is helpfulness to those in need of help; for what we do for others, the Holy Spirit will do for us. "Whoever would be great must be the minister of all" (146:36–37).

If we enter into silence we can meet God and become filled with wisdom, light, love, and power (40:3). We always carry within ourselves this secret place where we can meet God. It does not matter where we live, whether it is in a mountain, valley, marketplace or the quiet of our home; we can immediately, at any time, enter into that silence and find the house of God; it is within our soul. However, we shall find it easier to be away from the noise of business and the words and thoughts of men if we will go alone into the countryside. Especially when we are under a lot of pressure, it is better to go out and seek a quiet place to pray and meditate (40:6–10). In order to find this silence of the soul we must purify our hearts and lay aside all mental tension and all business cares, all fears, doubts, and troubled thoughts. Our wills must be absorbed by the divine; then we will come into a consciousness of holiness (40:12–14).

God never fails to notice any prayer or fast. He is there within the silence, and He blesses all our efforts (94:17). If we ask firmly, we shall receive; if we seek trustingly, we shall find; if we knock earnestly, the door will open. Everything belongs to us, and if we ask like a child and not like a beggar, we will be satisfied (137:14–15). The answer to our prayers may not appear completely right away, but we must not be discouraged, we are to pray again and again, and God will hear (137:8–9).

Love

"He who loves not the Christ, which is the love of God, before all else, can never gain the prize of Spirit Consciousness" (122:41). Within the soul of man there is something called Spirit Consciousness which will enable him to see the real world. It is asleep and cannot be awakened until man welcomes the Holy Spirit, which knocks at the door of his soul; nor can It enter until man of his own free will opens wide the door. The secret to opening that door is purity in life, prayer, and holy thoughts (44:21–25).

Heaven is not a place; it is a state of mind. God never made a heaven nor a hell for man; we are creators, and we make our own (33:8–9).

When Jesus was baptized by John, a voice from heaven said, "This is the well-beloved son of God, the Christ, the love of God made manifest" (64:13), but later Jesus said:

> Men call me Christ, and God has recognized the name; but Christ is not a man. The Christ is universal love, and Love is king. This Jesus is but man who has been fitted by temptations overcome, by trials multiform, to be the temple through which Christ can manifest to men. . . . Look not upon the flesh; it is not king. Look to the Christ within, who shall be formed in every one of you, as he is formed in me. When you have purified your hearts by faith, the king will enter in, and you will see his face (68:11–14). This king is love, and when this love becomes the greatest power in life, it is the Christ; so Christ is king. And everyone may have this Christ dwell in his soul, as Christ dwells in my soul (71:6–7).

We are all related, each one a part of the great human heart (51:17). If we are not kind to every form of life, to humans, animals, birds, and insects, we cannot expect the blessings of God, for as we give to others, so God will give to us (74:24).

Causes of Disease

It is often stated in the New Testament that when Jesus healed someone he frequently implied that the disease had been caused by the sin of the sick person. This is also the case in *The Aquarian Gospel*. For example, after healing a man who had been ill for 38 years and could not move without someone to help him, Jesus said, "Behold you are made whole; from henceforth guard your life aright; go on your way and sin no more, or something worse may fall on you" (91:21–22). On one occasion he talked about repressed anger as a cause of disease, "A curse is poison to the inner man, and if you hold and swallow down a curse it never will digest; it will poison every atom of your soul" (105:31).

He also talked about guilt and the difference in the result between offending another human and offending the Holy Spirit. In the case of the former we may be pardoned and our guilt cleansed by acts of kindness and of love. However, if we sin against the Holy Spirit by disregarding her when she tries to open up the doors of life for us, or by closing the windows of our soul when she would pour the light of love into our hearts and cleanse them with the fires of God, our guilt will not be eliminated now. We would have to wait for ages until the Holy Spirit opened up the doors of our life again (105:31–38).

In discussing fear Jesus said, "Fear is the chariot in which man rides to death" (52:15). One day a man who was possessed by violence and lust was brought to Jesus, who told him that his own deeds and evil thoughts had created all his problems, but he had to solve them for himself (83:7). Another man who was obsessed by evil spirits was cleansed of them by Jesus, who then told him to keep his mind fully occupied with good, and then the evil spirits would not be able to return. "They only come to empty heads and hearts" (89:15–21).

Unresolved grief is today recognized as a cause of disease, so comments by Jesus on this topic are interesting. One day he spoke to a grieving woman whose only son had just died. He told her to dry her eyes because she was grieving over an empty shell:

> You weep because your son is dead. Death is a cruel word; your son can never die. He had a task assigned to do in garb of flesh; he came; he did his work, and then he laid the flesh aside; he did not need it more. Beyond your human sight he has another work to do, and he will do it well, and then pass on to other tasks, and, by and by, he will attain the crown of perfect life. And what your son has done, and what he yet must do, we all must do (54:6–9).

He went on to say that if she continued to grieve, her sorrow would increase daily and absorb her very life until eventually she would be nothing but grief; also, that her great grief was making her son grieve, whereas he needed her comfort now as he always had. She should cheer up and lose herself in helping others dry their tears (54:10–12).

Another time, when Jesus was traveling in India prior to his baptism, someone brought word to him that his father, Joseph, had died and that his mother grieved and longed to see Jesus once again. Jesus then wrote her a letter in which he said that all was well for her and his father, whose earthly work was completed. She was to stop crying, because tears cannot conquer grief or mend a broken heart. It is idle to grieve; busy people do not grieve, they have no time for it. When grief arises, we are advised to lose ourself in the ministry of love and give our life for those who live, and grief will disappear (30:6–15).

Death

Many who desire to be healed, or to heal others, feel that death represents failure; so Jesus' comments on death are of great value. One time, while he was on the way to heal a very sick child, he was told that it had died. He said:

> What is death? It is the passing of the soul out of the house of flesh. Man is the master of the soul and of its house. When man has risen up from doubt and fear, lo, he can cleanse the empty house and bring the tenant back again.

He then restored life to the child (120:13–15, 25–32).
Another time he said:

> Death does not mean the end of life. The grave is not the goal of men, no more than is the earth the goal of seeds. Life is the consequence of death. The seed may seem to die, but from its grave the tree arises into life. So man may seem to die, but he lives on, and from the grave he springs up into life (155:16–18). Except a grain of wheat fall into earth and die it can be nothing but a grain of wheat; but if it die it lives again, and from its grave a hundred grains of wheat arise. (156:31).

After Jesus had been seen by the three disciples talking to Moses and Elijah before his death, he told the disciples that those men had come so that the disciples would know that heaven and earth and the occupants of both planes are one. The veil that separates the two worlds is very thin, and if we purify our hearts by faith, the veil will be removed and we shall see that death is an illusion (129:18–19).

After his death and resurrection, Jesus appeared to the master priests in Egypt and told them that the essence of the resurrection of the dead is in the physical body, and when it is quickened by the Holy Spirit, the body will be raised to a higher vibration and become like the bodies on the spirit plane, which we cannot see. However, the body has first to disintegrate, and then God breathes on it and life springs forth from death—and the physical body is changed to a divine form. "The will of man makes possible the action of the Holy Breath. When will of man and will of God are one, the resurrection is a fact" (178:36–41).

Reincarnation

Jesus also discussed Karma as a cause of disease. He said that men are diseased and deformed because they once transgressed the laws of perfect life, and every law of God must be fulfilled. They may escape the punishment that seems proper for their crimes in this life; but every deed and word and thought creates its own results. If a wrong is done, the person who did the wrong has to make it right. Only when all the wrongs have been redeemed will man be at one with God (114:48–51).

We cannot look upon a single life and know that person's karma. We must understand the law that "Results depend on Cause." Men are not specks of dust floating about in the air of one short life and then lost in nothingness. We are undying parts of the eternal whole that come and go many times between the earth and the spirit plane in order that we may grow. A cause may originate in one life and the results become apparent in another (114:26–30).

One day, seeing a man who had been blind from birth, Peter asked that if disease and imperfections are all caused by sin, did the man or did his parents sin? Jesus answered:

> Afflictions all are partial payments on a debt, or debts, that have been made. There is a law of rec-

> ompense that never fails, and it is summarized in that true rule of life: "Whatsoever man shall do to any other man, some other man will do to him. . . . Affliction is a prison cell in which a man must stay until he pays his debts unless a master sets him free that he may have a better chance to pay his debts. . . . Behold we may make free this man that he may better serve the race and pay his debts (138:2–17).

Thus Jesus said that karma can be paid by service in lieu of suffering.

5

SETH

OVER THE PAST 20 years Seth has dictated all or part of at least six books through a trance medium named Jane Roberts, who died in 1984. Seth calls himself an "energy personality essence" and appears to be a discarnate entity—that is, one who has lived on this planet in a human body many times and now lives on the Spirit plane. Scattered throughout the first three books (listed in the footnote and amounting to more than 1300 pages) there are several references to healing. It is from these books that the following teachings have been extracted and summarized.

In her introduction to the third book, Jane Roberts says, "I had to read the manuscript to find out what was in it," because it was dictated entirely by Seth while Roberts was in a trance state. The books themselves contain a great deal of information about human life on this planet and life in the Spirit World, and they are well worth reading in full.

THE SETH MATERIAL; SETH SPEAKS; and THE NATURE OF PERSONAL REALITY: A SETH BOOK, by Jane Roberts, are published by Prentice-Hall Inc., Englewood Cliffs, NJ 07632.

Healing

The essence of the teaching on healing transmitted by Seth is that our entire physical environment and body are the materialization of our beliefs. We create our own reality and experience in life by the way we think and believe. The images in our mind draw to themselves all the proper emotional energy and power needed to fill them out as physical events. It all originates within us and therefore can be changed in any way we want by changing our thoughts and beliefs.

We are constantly transforming our thoughts and emotions into physical form. We can obtain a clear picture of what is going on within us by looking at what is happening outside us. What seems to be an objective, concrete event independent from ourselves is actually the materialization of our inner emotions, energy, and thoughts. Therefore our physical body is created by us at each moment as a direct result of what we believe we are, and it changes in important chemical and electromagnetic ways as we constantly change our thoughts.

Thus our conscious thoughts and feelings regulate our health. We are in fact immune from disease as long as we believe that we are immune. The body and mind are a united, self-regulating healing system. Seth says that illnesses usually represent unfaced problems, and these dilemmas embody challenges meant to lead us to greater achievement and fulfillment. Because body and mind operate so well together, one will attempt to cure the other and will often succeed if left alone.

If we imagine dire circumstances, ill health, or desperate loneliness, these will be automatically materialized, for these thoughts themselves bring about the conditions that will give them reality in physical terms. If we want to have good health, Seth tells us to imagine this as vividly as, in fear, we imagined the opposite. He says:

> True self knowledge is indispensable for health or vitality. The recognition of the truth about the self

> simply means that you must first discover what you think about yourself subconsciously. If it is a good image, build upon it. If it is a poor one, recognize it as only the opinion you have held of yourself, and not as an absolute state, and therefore you can change it, if you wish to do so.

This teaching therefore means that we are 100 percent responsible for what we experience in our lives. Pain, disease, and bodily malfunction are purely the result of our own thoughts, emotions, and beliefs. That which exists physically existed first in thought and feeling. If we don't like our experience, we can alter the kind of messages that we are sending to our body and to friends and associates by means of our thoughts. Seth says that there is nothing in our exterior experience that did not originate within us. In the most miraculous fashion we are given the gift of creating our own experience. This means that even false beliefs will seem to be justified by physical happenings, since our experience in the outside world is the materialization of these beliefs.

All of the available data coming in to us is sifted, weighed and valued in a precise search for the material that will give physical emphasis to those beliefs. Information or events that are of the opposite point of view are ignored to a large degree, or are distorted in such fashion that they are made to fit in with what the mind *says* is reality. It is clear that we have complete control over what we believe; others may try to change those beliefs, but we make the choice. The majority opinion of those around us, or in the world as a whole, may hold differently, but we still make our own decision as to what *we* believe. This means that we cannot blame our parents, our childhood, our spouse, our children, our employer, or "fate" for what we experience. This can be rather terrifying; it is so much easier to say that it is "their" fault. On the other hand, it can be very liberating when we realize how much power we have over our own lives. But Seth does not leave it at that; he says much more that is helpful in this context.

We are born without any beliefs (except maybe some that are carried over from previous lives) but we develop them from the beliefs of our parents, friends, or teachers, accepting or rejecting them as we choose. We also accumulate them from the religion we adopt and from our experiences in life. In addition, we are born in the midst of certain mass beliefs of our country and the world.

We are conscious beings who inherently contain creative faculties that enable us to change matter because it receives its vitality from our thoughts. Creativity and experience are being formed moment by moment by each individual according to his beliefs. If we dwell upon physical limitations that we believe we have, then we shall experience these in our lives. We are told to create a new picture in our mind, different from the one the physical senses are currently showing, in exactly the area where change is required. Then we are to concentrate on those thoughts that produce the results that we want. In *almost* all cases of present limitation we have schooled ourselves to stress negative aspects. Our beliefs *can* build barriers that limit our experience. We are urged to be convinced that we can alter our beliefs, and to be willing to try.

Seth says that we choose even the kind of illness that we have, according to the nature of our beliefs. Each of us knows the time of our death, but even such decisions can be altered at any time in the "Now." No one dies who has not made the decision to do so, and no disease is accepted blindly. The entire body can be regenerated in a way that would be impossible to predict in usual medical terms.

If we accept these ideas but at the same time live with a disease or some other experience that we desire to change, how do we go about it? Seth has some advice for us on that too. First, we need to realize that our body has an overall body consciousness filled with energy and vitality. It automatically corrects any imbalances if it is allowed to do so by our beliefs. Each part of our body believes what we tell it about itself. Within the body and mind, each problem contains its own solution if it is honestly faced.

Each symptom, mental or physical, is a clue to resolving the conflict behind it. Thus every illness contains within it the seeds of its own healing.

Seth says:

> If you have a physical symptom do not run away from it. Feel its reality in your body. Let the emotions follow freely. These will lead you, if you allow them to flow, to the beliefs that caused the difficulty.

Imagination and emotion are the most concentrated forms of energy that we possess as physical creatures. Any strong emotion carries within it far more energy than is required to send a rocket to the moon. Imagination can propel ideas in the direction that we desire. To act independently of physical reality as it appears to us, we are advised to begin to initiate action that we want to occur in our body or physical experience by creating it in our being. This is done by combining our belief, emotion, and imagination, and forming them into a mental picture of the desired physical result.

For example, remember to recognize resentment if we feel it, and know that we can eliminate it. Having recognized it, we can then imagine pulling it out by the roots and replacing it with a positive feeling. However, we have to imagine this removal process. This is the difference between repression and positive action. In repression the resentment is pushed down and ignored; but Seth's way is to recognize it, imaginatively pull it out as being undesirable, and replace it with thoughts of peace and constructive energy.

Seth says we are not our emotions; they flow through us, we feel them, and then they disappear. When we attempt to hold them back, we build them up like mountains. Our nervous system reacts spontaneously when we allow it to. It is only when we try to deny our emotions that they become dangerous. Seth goes on to say:

> All illness is momentarily accepted by the personality as a part of the self—here lies its danger. It is not just symbolically accepted, and I am not speaking in symbolic terms. An impeding action such as an illness is quite literally accepted by the personality structure, and once this occurs a conflict develops.
>
> The self does not want to give up a portion of itself, even while that portion may be painful or disadvantageous. There are many reasons behind this. For one thing, while pain is unpleasant, it is also a method of familiarizing the self against the edges of quickened consciousness. Any heightened sensation, pleasant or not, has a stimulating effect upon consciousness to some degree. Even when the stimulus may be humiliatingly unpleasant, certain portions of the psychological structure accept it indiscriminately because it is a sensation, and a vivid one. This acquiescence to even painful stimuli is a basic part of the nature of consciousness. Action does not differentiate between pleasant, painful or joyful stimuli.

Seth also says that all illness is almost always the result of some action that cannot be pursued. When the action is allowed, the illness will vanish. However, the action that was blocked may be one with disastrous consequences which the illness may prevent. He also distinguishes between physical illnesses that are observable to the outsider and illnesses with hidden symptoms, such as an ulcer. The former are the end product of a process of discovery—inner problems have been brought out where they can be faced and conquered. In the case of interior symptoms, it is a sign that the person is not yet willing to face the problem.

If an individual is ill, they are advised to suspend the current negative belief that they are ill for five to ten minutes every day. They are instead deliberately to hold to a belief that they are well, concentrating intently on the health that is desired and using visualization and verbal thought. They can pretend that they are under hypnosis, with themselves as hypnotist and subject. During that time, desire and belief will be one. Then, once a day they should act as though they were not sick, and with complete belief that this is so, being absolutely in the "now" moment with no thought of the past or the future. This will sometimes bring literally awesome results. At other times we are urged to concentrate on our accomplishments, successes, and positive aspects. This will by itself operate in a constructive fashion and build up our own sense of worth and power.

If we follow these directions and understand their meaning, we will find the results most startling and effective. Energy may be directed to any portion of the body, and if we do not block its action by disbelief, that portion will be cured. However, it is vital that we realize that we are working with beliefs in the mind and that the real work is done there. We ought not to look for immediate physical results. They will follow *as surely and certainly* as the "bad" results followed. We are to believe that the good results will come but are not to check constantly for them. Within a month the new condition will materialize.

Diseases can be eliminated, even those that seem fatal, but only if the beliefs behind them are erased or altered enough so that their specific focussing effect upon the body is sufficiently released. When we accept beliefs that contradict each other, the signals given to our body and inner self are a jumble of counter-directions. These set off alarms; the body will not function properly, or the overall emotional environment will suffer. These are meant to be taken as a sign that change is needed.

The inner self keeps the body alive but looks to the conscious mind for its assessment of the body's condition and reality, and it forms the image in line with the conscious mind's beliefs. On an unconscious level we organize the atoms and molecules that make up the cells that form our body, by changing our beliefs in spite of evidence that conflicts. Our beliefs create the blueprint. Unfortunately, our beliefs in disease are often reinforced by our doctor's own belief in disease as a reality, which is given great weight because we believe the doctor has greater wisdom and knowledge.

Molecules and atoms and even smaller particles have a condensed consciousness. They form into cells and form individual cellular consciousness. This combination results in a consciousness that is capable of much more experience and fulfillment than would be possible for the atom or molecule by itself. Thus each cell of the body has a separate intelligence or consciousness of its own, and each organ possesses the combined consciousness of all the cells it contains. There is a conscious cooperation between the cells in each organ, and between the organs themselves. Therefore, the living entity of our body is composed of other living entities each with its own right to fulfillment and existence. This inner consciousness forms the body by magically transforming thoughts and emotions into physical counterparts. Our body's condition perfectly mirrors our subjective state at any given time. Using atoms and molecules, we build our own body, forming basic elements into a form that we call our own.

Suppose, though, that we accept all the above but are not aware of what our beliefs really are—what do we do then? Seth says that our emotions will always lead us into a realization of our beliefs if we do not block them. Emotional states are always forces for action meant to be physically expressed. By going along with our feelings we unify our emotional, mental and physical states. If we try to fight or deny them we divorce ourselves from the reality of our being. Any emotion will change into another if we experience it honestly; we will become aware of the conscious system of beliefs behind the block and we will realize that we feel a certain way because we believe an idea that causes and justifies such a reaction.

Having uncovered a belief that we want to change, Seth suggests that we accomplish this by generating the emotion opposite to the one that arises from the belief that we want to change and that we reverse the direction of our imagination from the one dictated by the belief. At the same time we are consciously to assure ourself that the unsatisfactory belief is an idea about reality and not an aspect of reality itself. If we consciously and sincerely try to change a belief but find after some time that there has been no change in our outer experience, then we need to dig deeper. Underneath the belief that we consciously changed, there may be another belief that is even more powerful and controlling of our reality. For example, underneath a belief that we will always have allergies (which we change into a belief that we will always be healthy), there may be a deep conviction of our own unworthiness. Nothing will change in our outer experience until that belief is also changed.

Dreams are one of our greatest and most efficient natural therapies. Dreams constantly alter the chemical balance within our bodies. They may fill the body with needed hormones and provide an unpressured interlude. Dreams are the inner framework in which much of our physical body-building actually takes place. We have within ourselves the condensed knowledge of our entire being. This information cannot appear in any complete fashion within a consciousness connected with a physical brain. In the dreaming state, when the conscious mind is silenced, glimpses of the multidimensional self can appear in dream images that symbolically express our total being.

An interesting use of visualization is suggested by Seth. He says we can request that the thought content of our mind be translated into an intense image symbolically representing individual thoughts and the overall mental picture of our belief system. We should then take out what we do not like and replace it with more positive images. This does not mean that the inner picture must always be perfect, but it does mean that it should be well balanced. We can correct a physical condition in this manner, but if we examine our inner thoughts, we will find the source that initially brought about the illness. Sickness and suffering are not placed upon us by God or by any outside agency. They are a by-product of the learning process, created by us, in themselves quite neutral. They appear because we have misdirected the creative energy. However, they are a part of the creative force and come from the same source as health and vitality.

Seth discourages the use of medical drugs. He says that when imbalances of a physical nature are removed by the use of drugs, the body signals say that the inner conflict must have been taken care of also—while this may not be the case at all. The whole organism is not at one with itself under such conditions; the problem will merely manifest in a different way. On the other hand, if left alone, any chemical upsets in the body will naturally right themselves after the inner causes are removed by any of a variety of God-given healing methods.

There is inexhaustible energy available to each of us. It is electromagnetic by nature and is so powerful that even the most permanent-seeming condition of our lives can be changed. The atoms of our bodies and the particles that make up these atoms are in constant rapid motion, creating great exchanges of energy at all times. It is well known to the medical profession that the cells that consist of these atoms and particles are literally dying and being completely replaced all the time.

Our bodies have sound, light, and electromagnetic properties that we are not aware of, but which are even more susceptible to our thoughts and emotions than the physical structure of the body. Our ideas and thoughts have electromagnetic realities and regulate our health. Our feelings have electromagnetic realities that rise outward and affect the very atmosphere itself. However, because our ideas and beliefs have this electromagnetic reality, the constant interplay between strongly contradictory beliefs (the old ones that we desire to change and the new ones that we visualize) can cause great power blocks, impeding the flow of inner energy outward.

When we change our beliefs, circuits within the nervous system are changed, and energies that we do not understand seek out new connections on much deeper levels far beyond consciousness. The many involuntary and yet essential functions of the body perfectly mirror our consciously held ideas and beliefs. Likewise, the form of the body will accurately materialize in flesh those same ideas and beliefs. Our body is our most intimate feedback system, changing with our thoughts and experiences, and manifesting the physical counterpart of our thoughts.

Now Is the Point of Power

When can we make these changes? Seth says "NOW." This moment represents the point of our power through which we can affect both past and future events. If we learn to get hold of this feeling of power now, we can use it most effectively to alter our life situation in whatever way we choose. Seth emphasizes that this is the most important practical point in his teaching. If we must look at the past, we should look at the pleasures, accomplishments, and successes, not the negative events; otherwise we will reinforce the negative experiences from which we wish to escape. We can examine the past for evidence of what is wanted in terms of positive experience. Imagine the future from the power point of the present, remembering that the unconscious accepts those orders given to it by the conscious mind.

Death

Seth says that there is no separate, indivisible, specific point of death. Life is a state of becoming, and death is a part of this process of becoming. We are alive now, a consciousness knowing itself, sparkling with cognition amid a debris of dead and dying cells. We are very much alive while the atoms and molecules of our body die and are reborn. Our consciousness may withdraw from the body slowly or quickly, according to many variables. The environments that we shall experience after death are not somber at all. In fact, they are generally far more intense and joyful than our experience on this planet. A suicide may bring about his own death because he rejects existence on any but highly specific terms chosen by himself. If this is the case, Seth says he will have to learn differently. However, many others choose to deny experience while living a physical life, committing suicide quite as effectively without a physical death.

Reincarnation

Seth frequently mentions Reincarnation. He makes it very clear that we live many earthly lives, in each of which we experience conditions that we have chosen beforehand, circumstances and challenges tailored to fit our own needs and develop our own abilities. Thus a disease or a physical handicap sometimes may have originated as a result of actions taken in previous lives. This is commonly known as Karma, but Karma does not mean punishment. Seth says that "karma presents the opportunity for development. It enables the individual to enlarge understanding through experiences, to fill in gaps of ignorance, to do what should be done."

> Free will is always involved. If you hate another person, that hate may bind you to him through as many lives as you allow the hate to consume you. You draw to yourself in this existence, and in all others, those qualities upon which you concentrate your attention. If you vividly concern yourself with

> the injustices you feel have been done to you, then you attract more such experiences, and if this goes on, then it will be mirrored in your next existence. If you hate illness you may bring upon yourself a succeeding life of illness, because the hate has drawn it to you. If instead you expand your sense of love, of health and life, then you are drawn in this life, and in others, toward those qualities because they are those upon which you concentrate.

If we have no sympathy for those who are ill, then in our next life we may be born with a serious disease, which we have chosen, and find ourselves meeting those attitudes that once were ours, and thus develop compassion. However, such a life would also usually include other lessons such as a measure of discipline enabling one to use deeper abilities that were ignored in the life of good health. Actually Seth goes one step further than this. He claims that all our lives are lived simultaneously because in Reality there is no time, no past, present or future—all is now. As a result, our lives are open-ended, and the so called "cause" in one life and the "result" in the next are both happening at the same time, and therefore one is not dependent on the other. We form our reality now in our present and can therefore change any so-called result now. We can restructure our "reincarnated past" in the same way that we can restructure the past in the present life, which only exists as a conscious or subconscious memory.

Individuals have often chosen birth defects or lifetime diseases as incentive for growth and creativity. However, whenever someone realizes that his point of power is in the present, he will not need a barrier to test himself against or to focus him. Such a life may also be chosen to experience something entirely new. For example, a person with several existences stressing intellectual achievement and repressing emotions might purposely decide upon a life in which mental abilities were extremely limited and the emotions allowed a full play. In other cases the incapacitated person will have accepted that life for personal reasons, but also as a role for the family as a whole. If highly intelligent parents place a great value upon intellect at the expense of emotions, then their retarded child may be acting out for them the emotional spontaneity of which they are so afraid in themselves.

6

SAINT GERMAIN

THE GREAT ASCENDED MASTER Saint Germain is one of those Powerful Cosmic Beings from the Great Host of Ascended masters who govern this planet. About 50 years ago he appeared to Guy W. Ballard (who wrote under the pen name of Godfrey Ray King) and gave him Transcendent Instruction and Teaching, which culminated in a series of books. The first two of them describe various events that Guy Ballard experienced, leading to his contact with Saint Germain, and include teachings by Saint Germain from time to time. The third book, *The "I AM" Discourses*, consists entirely of teaching by Saint Germain and four short discourses by Jesus.

From these teachings, those sections have been paraphrased or quoted which specifically refer to Spiritual or Cosmic Healing or the cause of disease. Unlike most of the other writings analysed for this book, these teachings were

ORIGINAL UNVEILED MYSTERIES and THE MAGIC PRESENCE, by Godfrey Ray King, and THE "I AM" DISCOURSES, by Saint Germain, are published by Saint Germain Press Inc., 1120 Stonehedge Drive, Schaumburg, IL 60194.

apparently not channeled by thought from some invisible spirit being, but rather Saint Germain actually appeared in an etheric body that Guy Ballard could see and hear. These books contain a tremendous amount of wonderful spiritual teaching and are well worth studying in full.

Healing

Saint Germain has a number of interesting points to make about Cosmic Healing. He says that Light is the Central Point of Life within every atom that comprises all physical manifestation. If we consciously envelop any person, place, condition, or thing in the Dazzling White "Light," we are penetrating the atomic structure into the Electronic, in which there is no imperfection. Then the object of our attention is brought forth as Perfect. This "Light" is always directed by thought, but it is imperative that all learn to control and direct it consciously. We are urged always to remember that "one becomes that upon which he meditates," and since all things have come forth from the "Light," "Light" is the Supreme Perfection and control of all things. Nothing is impossible. The "Light" never fails.

Saint Germain also says:

> When an individual sincerely uses affirmation, he brings about a full acceptance of the Truth of whatever he affirms, for its use is but to focus the attention of the outer mind so steadily upon the Truth, that he accepts it fully in his feelings, because feeling is the actual God-Energy released, which manifests the Truth affirmed. The continued use of affirmation brings one to the point where he has such a deep realization of the Truth in anything he affirms that he is no longer conscious of it as an affirmation. There is but One Source and Principle of Life to which we should give our undi-

> vided attention and that is the God Self within every individual.

Our ego needs to give conscious recognition to this God-Self at all times and keep in constant inner communion with It, no matter what the outer activity of our mind is. This Mighty God-Self within us is the Supreme Ruler of all creation and the only dependable Source of help in existence.

Whatever needs to be changed in our physical experience can be changed by calling our "Mighty I AM Presence" into action with our mind and body, and the result will always be produced without suffering or discord of any kind. "The Way of Perfection, which is the activity of the 'I AM Presence,' never demands of the personal self anything but the letting go of its chains, its discords, its limitations and its sufferings; and this change is always brought about harmoniously and through Divine Love." One way to heal the physical body is to

> call your "Mighty I AM Presence" to pour through your mind and body its Violet Consuming Flame. Then spend a few moments, at least three times a day, visualizing yourself standing within a pillar of Violet Flame rushing from the feet to some distance above the head and extending for at least three feet on each side around the body. Hold this picture, as long as you can comfortably do so; and feel the flame which is the Purifying Power of Divine Love, penetrating every cell of your body. This dissolves all impure and unnecessary substances in the cells of the body, thus clearing and illuminating the consciousness.

"With God all things are possible." Saint Germain says that we can so raise our consciousness into the Pure Essence of God that "all things with US are possible" as soon as we learn to direct this Gigantic Power by the Love and Wisdom of our own "Mighty I AM Presence." Those in the spirit world wonder why we are content to go through the experience of death, while all the time we cling to youth, beauty and Life; and yet we refuse to keep harmonious enough to let life be maintained.

We can renew any nerve or organ, and rebuild any part of the body into its Perfection almost immediately, if we declare with sufficient intensity that "I AM the Mighty Electronic Energy flowing through, filling and renewing every cell of my mind and body—right now." If, at first, we do not feel any great force pass over us, it does not mean that we have not received this Mighty Energy. If we will hold the thought that " 'I AM' the Perfect Activity of every organ and cell of my body," then it must manifest. If some organ seems to manifest pain or disease, we should instantly declare: "I AM the only and Perfect Energy acting there." Then every appearance of disturbance will be instantly corrected. We can positively produce whatever we want in our body, if we will fix our attention upon the Perfection of it and do not let our attention rest on its imperfections.

The Healer

If we see a disease or malfunction in someone else and say nothing, it is even worse than if we commented on it aloud, for it allows the problem to grow. When we cannot avoid seeing the situation, we should simply say to our "I AM Presence": "There is the 'I AM Presence' within that person, and with the human I am not concerned." It does not matter if it is a person or an inanimate object, the moment we see an imperfection, we are forcing that quality into our own experience.

We cannot deny the fact that all the energy we use comes from the God-Self, no matter how that energy is used. We are never to let any desire for service deprive us of our need to fix our undivided attention on our God-Self within. We will then naturally give the right service and do the right thing. The Law of True Divine Service always says to the personal self, "Thou shalt have no other gods before me." If we gain sufficient understanding, it is possible to cause our body to respond instantly to the higher and unlimited use of the "I AM Presence" within. Our body is an instrument through which we can let Life flow knowing no limitation nor defeat in anything. Alternatively, we can let thoughts and feelings of limitation and discord sent out by other people affect us.

Saint Germain says that those who offer their service in the Name of the Ascended Jesus Christ will always receive more than ordinary sustaining power. On one occasion Jesus appeared with Saint Germain and spoke to the assembled group as follows:

> In my ministry to mankind among the hills of Judea, preceding all conscious healing upon my part, within my own mind I was always conscious that: " 'I AM' the only Healing Presence" and, as that "Unlimited I AM Presence," I had the Right, the Power and the Ability, through that Presence, to command all outer activity of the mind to be silent and obey its Command. Thus when I spoke to individuals, I spoke with that Authority of the "I AM Presence," which I recognized as the Only Intelligence and Power acting or that could act. Within each one of you is the same "Mighty I AM Presence" which I used to accomplish the *Perfection* of that Mighty Presence. This seemed to humanity at that time, the performing of miracles. However, I assure you it was but consciously setting into action and use, Cosmic Laws that are ever about you to be set into activity through conscious direction. I tell you sincerely from My own Experience that *we must acknowledge the One Presence, Intelligence and Power; then, claim It as*

> *our own in our every thought and activity.* It is the only way this Mighty Perfection can be brought into the outer appearance and the fullness of your use.

Saint Germain emphasizes the limitless power that is available to us. He urges us to realize fully that God's intent is for every one of His children to have abundance of every good and perfect thing. He created Perfection and endowed us, His children, with exactly the same power as His. So we can create and maintain Perfection also, and we can express God-Dominion over the earth and everything in it. The power that enables us to do this is the energy of the God-Self that is within each of us. This limitless energy is flowing ceaselessly through our nervous system and is the Eternal Life and vitality in our bloodstream. If only we realized what freedom, power, and Light wait for us dependent *only* on our recognition and use of the Great Loving "Presence" Within! If we could only *feel* the closeness and *reality* of the Great "Presence" deeply, even for a moment, nothing could ever stand between us and the same wonderful works that Jesus and other Ascended Masters have attained. However, it is necessary to discipline our outer faculties and make them obedient to our Conscious Command of Perfection; we can then let this Tremendous Power flow through us without obstruction and use it constructively.

Forgiveness

Another important element in healing and spiritual life is forgiveness. Saint Germain speaks about it this way:

> An activity that will always bring Complete Freedom, is for an individual to pour out Unconditional and Eternal Forgiveness to everybody and everything. This does what nothing else can do

> to free everyone, as well as the person who sends it out. Forgiveness fills all with Light's Perfection. When Forgiveness is sincere, the individual will find his world reordered, as if by magic, and filled with every good thing. But remember that unless a discord is forgotten, it is not forgiven; because you cannot loose it or release yourself from it, until it is out of your consciousness. So long as you remember an injustice, or a disturbed feeling, you have not forgiven either the person, or the condition.

When the forgiveness is complete, we will feel serene and happy.

If we wish to seek revenge against anyone who has harmed us, whether this is imaginary or not, we will cause injury to our mind and body. We hold on to the things we do not want by allowing our minds to dwell upon discordant things from the past that cannot be helped by our physical senses.

> In any wrong condition the first thing to do is to call on the Law of Forgiveness. The correct way to call this Law into action is to say: "I AM the Law of Forgiveness and the Consuming Flame of all inharmonious action and human consciousness.

Saint Germain says that forgiveness must come before healing can be permanent. God never criticizes or condemns us, no matter what mistakes we have made, but every time we fall He says, "Arise my child and try again, and keep on trying until at last you have attained the True Victory and Freedom of your God-given Dominion." When we are conscious of having made a mistake, our first act should always be to call on the Law of Forgiveness and demand wisdom and strength not to make the same mistake a second time.

Love

Saint Germain, like all other Master Teachers, maintains that Love is an indispensable element in Healing. The fundamental principle upon which all Perfection rests is Love. The transcendent and magnificent activities of Love and Light are the natural outcome of God's creation and are manifested when we obey His command "to Love." When we look away from Love, we are deliberately and consciously choosing the experience of chaos, which is certain to follow. Anyone who seeks to exist without Love cannot survive long anywhere in creation. "This is the Law of Universal, as well as individual Life. It is Immutable, Irrevocable, Eternal yet Beneficent, for creation in form exists that God may have something upon which to pour out *Love* and so express in action."

Our own miscreations drive us on continually until we are willing to understand Life and obey its *One Law*—Love. None of us escapes this action, and it continues until our ego asks the reason for its misery and finally understands that its release from the experience of suffering can only come through obedience to the "Law of Love": "Love alone is the basis of harmony and the right use of all Life energy."

Love is the "Active Principle of God." When we are loving, we surround what we are loving with the Radiant Presence and Activity of God. Once we become really aware that "God is Love," and that the True Activity of love comes through the heart, we will understand that to focus our attention on the desire to Love, for any given purpose, is a supreme privilege. "Love is the First Principle of Life and may be generated to any degree, or without any limit whatsoever, for Infinite use." This means conscious devotion to the outpouring of this limitless Fountain of Love, which is the heart of our Being and the Heart of the Universe.

Whatever our conscious attention is firmly fixed upon, that quality becomes part of our experience: "Whatever an individual sees with deep feeling within another individual, *he forces into his own experience.*" This is why the only desirable feeling for us to radiate is the Presence of Divine, Pure, Unselfish Love:

> Through the conscious action of the individual, Divine Love, consciously directed, becomes Love, Wisdom and Power in action. This is why Divine Love, consciously directed to accomplish things, produces such marvelous results. It becomes Instantaneous and All-powerful as soon as the outer consciousness ceases to limit It.
>
> Divine Love, being the Heart of Infinity and of the Individual, is an Ever-flowing Intelligent Flame that releases Energy, Wisdom, Power and Substance without limit. It will release Boundless blessings to all who will harmonize their own personalities enough to let it come through.

The more we understand Life and Perfection, the simpler life becomes; and finally we need to do only one thing, which is constantly to fill our thoughts and feelings with Divine Love. Divine Love is the most Invincible Power of the Universe. If we use it without limit, nothing will be impossible to us, and it will be perfect protection against anything that might harm us.

Causes of Disease

The only cause of our physical experience in life is the way we think and the way we feel, and therefore to experience Perfect Order our mind and emotions must be corrected and controlled. The Eternal Law of Life is: "What you think and feel you bring into form; where your thought is there you are, for you are your consciousness; and what you meditate upon you become." If we allow our minds to dwell upon thoughts of hate, condemnation, lust, envy, jealousy, criticism, fear, doubt, or suspicion, and if we allow these feelings to generate within us, we shall certainly experience discord, failure, and disaster. As long as we persist in allowing our attention to be held by such thoughts—whether they be about nations, persons, places, conditions, or things—we are absorbing those activities into the substance of our mind, body, and affairs. In fact, we are forcing them into our experience.

> The feeling side of human nature is the feminine activity of consciousness, within every individual. The thought is the masculine activity of the mind. A thought never becomes dynamic in the outer life, until it passes through the feeling body. The feeling condenses upon the thought pattern, the atomic substance of the outer activity of Life. In thus passing through the feeling body, the thought becomes clothed, and thereafter exists as a separate living thing outside of the Individual's mind.

Saint Germain says that the feeling activity of Life is the most unguarded point of human consciousness and that the greatest crime in the Universe against the Law of Love is humanity's almost ceaseless sending forth of every kind of irritable and destructive feeling. Discordant feeling is the producer of conditions we call disintegration, old age, lack of memory, and every other failure in the world of human experience. The effect upon the body structure is the same as that produced upon a building if the mortar holding the bricks together were to receive repeated shocks, and each day these were increased. This continued shock would shake apart the particles composing the mortar, and the building would collapse into a chaotic mass.

We are advised to make the effort to eliminate discordant thoughts, feelings, and activities by freely controlling our minds in order to transcend these limitations permanently. No one can hope to rid his life and world of misery, discord, and destruction until he controls his own thoughts and feelings:

> Where Peace, Love and Light do not abide within the thoughts and feelings of a human being no amount of physical effort can possibly keep the outer-self expressing youth and beauty. Whatever discord the outer-self allows to flash through the thought and feeling is that instant stamped upon the flesh of the physical body. Thoughts and feelings are living, pulsating things. The individual who knows that will use his wisdom and control himself accordingly.

We alone choose and create the qualities and forms we wish to pour into our Life, for we are the only energizer of our world and all it contains. When we think or feel, part of our Life energy goes forth to sustain our creation. We have been given free will and choice, and we create in the world about us whatever we concentrate our thoughts upon. It is essential to understand that thoughts and *feelings* are the only Creative Powers in the Universe.

> The angry, condemning person, who sends out destructive thought, feeling or speech to another who is poised in his own God power, receives back to himself the quality with which he charged this power; while the poised person receives the energy which serves him, and which he automatically requalifies by his own poise. Thus the creator of discord through anger and condemnation is consciously destroying himself, his world of activity, and his affairs.

If we discriminate between our own thoughts—that is, thoughts from our inner being—and the suggestions made by other people and the evidence of the senses, which judge by appearances only, we will be able to avoid all discordant experiences. Each individual, by thought and feeling, has the power to rise to the highest or sink to the lowest. Each one of us determines our own experience; no one else does. By conscious control of what we allow our minds to accept, we can live in the Presence of God; or we can look away from God and become lower than the animals, sinking our human consciousness into oblivion. Outer harmony is essential if the fullness of the Inner Perfection and Power is to be expressed in outer life. The importance of maintaining a *feeling* of peace and love cannot be emphasized too strongly. For if we do this, the "Mighty God Presence Within" can act without limitation at once. We can only experience Divine Thoughts and Feelings by thinking upon *Divinity*; for like produces like throughout Infinity.

One more factor that is important in maintaining our health and healing ourselves is the matter of Free Will. Saint Germain reminds us that:

> Man is the Son of God. He is commanded by the Father to choose how he shall direct the Life energy, and what quality he wishes his fulfilled desire to express. This he *must* do for free will is his birthright. The personal self of every individual is endowed with the Power of Choice as to what it wishes to think, to feel, to create, and experience. If one uses all the substance and energy of his Being constructively, then Peace, Expansion, Joy, Opulence and Glory are the return unto Life for the Outpouring of Its Gifts. If one chooses to create otherwise, his misery and destruction return into himself and destroy his body.

To us, His Children, God has given free will and the ability to choose, and we need to understand that we are the only ones to decide what action shall be allowed in our lives and world. Thus God only acts in our lives and world in accordance with our decisions. It is most unfortunate that orthodox religion claims that God acts of His Own Free Will in the Life of an individual or nation, because this is definitely *not true*. God can only act through our minds. The personalities that we experience in ourselves and others are only vehicles for the use and expression of the Mighty Individuality of God, which is God's Will and our free will; but our free will only comes into use when we consciously direct it.

Even in cases of accident, we do not leave our body until we will to do so. "Everything that happens to the body is and will always be under the control of the individual's free will."

Saint Germain at various times mentions several other causes of disease. For example: (*a*) the most common is hatred or resentment of another individual; (*b*) trying to enjoy something through injustice will result in losing some faculty by which one could enjoy it; (*c*) jealousy opens the door to many destructive activities; (*d*) saying "I am sick" reverses the Principle of Life, which is naturally all Perfection. When we let an idea of imperfection, or separation from God, occupy our mind, a corresponding condition begins to express itself in our body and world. This causes us to feel separated from our Source. The moment we think ourselves separated from God, we think that our Life has a beginning and an end.

If someone deliberately takes the life of another human being, or mentally determines to take it, he has created the cause of his own death. Even a feeling or desire for the death of another person will do the same thing, because the feeling is projected out onto the other person and then starts to return to the one who sent it out. Many people cause their own death by this very subtle process, because no one ever escapes this Immutable Law:

> There is only One Law of Life, and that is "Love." The Self Conscious, thinking individual who will not, or who does not obey that Eternal, Beneficent

> Decree, cannot and will not retain the physical body because all that is not Love dissolves form, and it matters not whether it be thought, word, feeling or deed—intentional or unintentional—the Law acts regardless.

Saint Germain claims that the seed within man and woman is only intended for the sacred office of creating a body by which another soul may come into physical embodiment. At all other times the "Glorious Light within the body" should be raised into the top of the head and allowed to flow up in adoration unto the "Mighty I AM Presence." Instead of wasting the wonderful Liquid Light, the Marvelous God-given Essence of Life, in sex sensation and excesses—whereby the body becomes decrepit, flabby, crippled, the face lined, the eyes dull, the whole structure stooped and feeble, the brain inactive, sight and hearing impaired, and the memory unable to function—this energy should be rightly used in Wonderful, Idealistic, Creative Activity. Then the physical body would remain eternally youthful and beautiful, the brain and faculties keen, alert, and active, and the whole physical expression would become the Image and Likeness of the Living God—truly the "Temple of the Most High." If this Life Essence is released at the generative center for sex pleasure, instead of building a new physical embodiment for another soul, the process of disintegration of the physical body is started. This is the Inevitable, Inexorable Law of physical embodiment, and there is no person in the Universe who can change it.

Death

> From the Heart-center of God flows a stream of Life Essence, or Liquid Light which enters the physical body through the pineal gland, and fills the nerve channels. It flows through the nerves, as blood does through the veins. This beats the heart,

> moves the muscles of the body, and enables one to walk or raise the hand. It is also the Energizing Light within the brain cells. The reason the race continues to experience so called death is because of the waste of this Liquid Light through emotional excesses, instead of retaining It within the physical brain and body to rebuild the cellular structure and supply the Motive Power for the entire body. Man becomes that upon which his attention rests.

Saint Germain says that death is only an opportunity for rest and re-attunement of the faculties of the personal consciousness—that it frees individuals from the turmoil and discords of Earth long enough to receive an Inflow of Light and Strength, which will enable them to take up the work of physical experience again. Death is also a means of release from a vehicle which is of no further use for the Perfection of Life. When the physical body is so incapacitated that the personality occupying it can no longer make a self-conscious effort to express Perfection, then nature takes a hand in things and dissolves the body so that the individual may have a new chance to progress on the path.

It is selfish for us to grieve over the death of a loved one, and it retards the greater good the loved one should be enjoying. Grief from a sense of loss is really rebellion against the action of a Law that has seen fit to give another a greater opportunity for rest and growth:

> Nothing in the Universe goes backward, and all—no matter what the temporary appearance—is moving forward to greater and greater Joy and Perfection. In True, Divine Love there is no such thing as separation, and that which feels a sense of separation is not Love. When one thinks of a loved one who has passed on, he is really with that loved one in his Higher Mental Body the moment his consciousness is upon the other person.

The physical body is the receptacle into which God pours the Light, but only for a constructive purpose. When that purpose is continually interfered with, the Light is withdrawn and the physical body, which should be the Temple of the Most High Living God, disintegrates.

> It is amazing how humanity refuses to understand why the minds and bodies of the race continue to grow old, decay and disintegrate, when some of the most materialistic scientists acknowledge that the cell, of which the physical bodies are made up, is Eternally Immortal. The Cell contains within It the Power to eternally renew and sustain Itself because there is perfect balance in all its parts. If left to its own activity and sphere it will continue to maintain that Perfection.

Reincarnation

Saint Germain speaks of Reincarnation as a fact of eternal life:

> People must understand that they have lived over and over again in hundreds—sometimes thousands—of lives, each time in a new physical body. The Law of re-embodiment is the activity in human growth that gives the individual an opportunity to re-establish a balance in conditions that he has *consciously* caused to be thrown out of balance. It is but one activity of the Law of compensation—cause and effect, or what might be called an automatic balancing process, governing all forces everywhere in the Universe. The right understanding of this Law gives one the explanation of many conditions in human experience which otherwise seem wholly unjust. It is the only logical explanation for the infinite complexities and experiences of human creation, and reveals the operation and the Law

> upon which all manifestation rests. It makes one know that there is no such thing as chance or accident. All is under direct, exact and Perfect Law. Every experience of consciousness has a former cause, and everything at the same instant is the cause of a future effect.

However, we can consciously correct and overcome our mistakes by the Power of Divine Love. Thus we can avoid the necessity for compulsory balancing and purification by the Action of Cosmic Law. When we start to do wrong, we immediately set in motion the Cosmic Law of Retribution, and we can no more avoid retribution striking us sometime, somewhere, than we can stop the action of the planets. If we are the innocent victim of some harmful act by another, retribution sometimes seems a long time coming; but the more it is delayed, the more powerfully it acts when it does arrive. No one can avoid this Law.

Saint Germain tells us that the sense appetites of former lives become the driving forces and habits of succeeding ones, keeping us slaves of discord, lack, and necessity, propelling us through a multitude of human problems and experiences that we have created, finally *compelling* us to learn and obey the Law of the One—LOVE. We cannot escape this Law, and it continues until we consciously ask the reason for our misery, and understand that our release from the experience of suffering can only come through *obedience* to the "Law of Love." "Through Life after Life man continually meets his own creation, turned upon himself, until he builds his Universe according to the Pattern of Divine Perfection, which is the True Expression of his own Divinity." There is only one way we can avoid the necessity for reincarnation, and that is through a conscious effort to comprehend the Law of Life. This is accomplished by earnestly seeking, and making permanent, a conscious contact with the God within, and holding firmly to It in the face of every condition in the outer life.

7

GILDAS

RUTH WHITE is a medium in England who has been channeling information from a teacher or guide on the spirit plane for over twenty years. He calls himself Gildas (pronounced with a soft G), which means "A messenger of Truth." Ruth White says that she "sees" him dressed in a loose, white, monkish robe; he is dark with a young-looking face, and his expression is full of radiance and compassion. He is very tall, about six feet four inches; his voice is deep and mellow and often full of a gentle humor. He has warned listeners to try to resist the temptation to inquire about who he is. He says, "In the work it is the messages which are given that matter."

Healing

Gildas says that "All forms of healing have their place and, if used cooperatively, could bring about a great dif-

THE HEALING SPECTRUM and FURTHER GILDAS COMMUNICATIONS, by Ruth White and Mary Swainson, are published by The C.W. Daniel Co. Ltd., 1 Church Street, Saffron Walden, CB10 1JP, Essex, England.

ference in all aspects of the health of man at this time." Spiritual healings operate on all of a person's bodies, including the very subtle bodies as well as the mental and physical. If there is sickness, disharmony, or dysfunction at the physical level, this moves through all levels and has an effect on the whole system. Currently, healing is inadequate because only one area at a time is treated, so the restoration of harmony for the total being is very difficult. Some people put all their faith in orthodox medicine, whereas others tend to rely entirely on spiritual healers and counselors. Thus there is rarely the combination of methods that would result in a true and complete healing.

Gildas suggests that self-healing is very difficult, because the healer needs to be as detached as possible in order to obtain the maximum effectiveness of the healing energy. Only a few can detach themselves sufficiently from their own pains, illnesses, and problems to open themselves completely to the healing power. Thus we usually need another's help to channel the healing on our behalf. If we want to heal ourselves, we are advised to try to live wholly and harmoniously. The more important of these is wholeness, yet wholeness cannot be attained without harmony.

It is not easy to live and think harmoniously, but our goal should always be to live with such inner peace that the inevitable outer discords cannot have any lasting effect upon us. Then we shall find that we no longer need self-healing or healing from others, because we will be whole and healthy, and life will flow for us as it is intended to. Each small step towards this ideal is a step upon the path to complete self-healing and protection. Where our total being is in harmony, disease will not attack us, unless there are karmic reasons.

The Healer

Gildas says that anyone can be a channel for healing; the only qualities required are positive receptivity and acceptance:

> The will should be subdued as much as possible; you cannot force the healing to be accepted by an act of will; you can only act as a channel for a positive force. This force, flowing through you, will surround the patient and be available to him and, if he is able to respond, healing at one level or another will result.

Those who wish to become healers need only to offer themselves as a channel for healing to be put through them to the one who is sick. Many will find it easier than others for the healing energy to flow through them. This is usually because of training in previous incarnations. Everyone seeking to evolve is urged to endeavor to cultivate his natural healing ability so that it may be used for their fellow human beings.

It is the positive, conscious desire to be of service that helps people to become a channel for the healing power, and not any other particular qualities or abilities. We are never to underestimate our supreme importance in the Divine plan. We can be the spirits' contact and can enable them to achieve that which they cannot achieve alone. Instead of striving to raise ourselves and our vibrations in a tense sort of way with the mind alone, we can picture healing as something that we can relax into with the heart.

Gildas says that the fields where many are needed are the more spiritual ones, and there is a great need for those who have any form of spiritual awareness to begin to train and expand this awareness for the purpose of eventually using it for healing. Awareness needs developing if we wish to progress in becoming a channel, learning to extend our awareness and understanding beyond the physical or that which comes easily to us. By doing this, we can begin to understand that all is One. When we meditate, we are advised to concentrate upon the higher centers (chakras) and to learn to open and attune them to a peaceful sense of receptivity. Meditation and study will bring an expansion of awareness, but it also grows through a determination to hold ourselves open and tolerant to thought and experience. "Much learning comes from experience; therefore accept as much of experience as life brings to you; accept thoughts which you might tend to shut out, consider them, remain open minded, and a certain growth and expansion will take place."

As part of our learning we are urged to use every moment creatively.

> This may sound tiring or impossible, but creativity which is harmonious and rhythmic and springs from a true center feeds the creator, and the fountain of energy need never run dry once the secret is discovered and the necessary discipline applied.

Our highly trained minds can be a hindrance to us in this work; it is suggested that we concentrate more on feeling. Because the qualities of mind are valued and needed, we may find it hard to accept the necessity of developing, and even relying upon, feeling. However, with diligent and gradual work and growth this can be achieved.

The purpose of prayer in healing is to entrust sick or suffering individuals to the care of healing forces and healers from all sides. "The person who prays and intercedes for healing acts something like a medium through whom the healing waves may be concentrated for those who are in need." When we think about healing, Gildas says that it is extremely neceessary to carry with us throughout our thinking the concept of wholeness. Wholeness, oneness, and unity cannot be stressed too much. Sometimes after a healing has taken place, other symptoms or problems appear because the disease has not been tackled from the standpoint of wholeness.

It is good to acquire some technique or procedure for healing, since this occupies the conscious mind and thought and helps us to become as open and as receptive as possible. Also, in this respect, Gildas says that technique is as important to those working from the spirit plane as it can be to us, but the particular technique that is chosen is of very little significance to them in directing the healing force through us.

> Wherever there are those willing to act as channels, alone or in groups, and where the healing forces are called upon, there they will be. The flow of spiritual healing is at your service. The healing flow, although readily and easily available, can often be somewhat impeded by the would-be healer (often quite unconsciously) and sometimes by the very strength of the healer's desire to be used as an instrument for healing.

The important thing is the receptivity, relaxation, and detachment of the would-be channel.

Sometimes we may seek healing for a particular problem, and even though that problem may remain unchanged, some other positive change on another level may occur. We may or may not become aware of these changes. They may be mental ones, or the individual may become able to accept and overcome something which previously he had felt would never be possible, and thus he is helped along his particular karmic path:

> Sometimes by acting as a healing channel you may set in motion a long, slow process, very positive but to most invisible. When you seek to heal, the temptation on the part of both healer and patient is to look at the physical for results. This is understandable because your world is inevitably concerned and bound up with the physical and with matter; yet because of this limitation you may sometimes fail to understand that other levels *are* there, and are equally, if not more important.

As we learn to be healers, we are asked to seek always to know more about the concept of wholeness, and then we shall more easily be convinced that our healing prayers do not go unanswered.

> Nothing may show at the physical or even the mental level in the lifetime of the patient, but at the most subtle levels of his consciousness some small response may have been made which will then continue to permeate to every level, until in consciousness at some future time he comes into the knowledge of his own wholeness and spirituality.

Therefore as healers we need to accept the fact that we channel an energy that will have very positive effects, but not always at the level which we expect. We need also to accept that some of the healing force that we channel may not be accepted by the other person at any level, because he may not be karmically ready or able to accept. However, this positive force is never wasted; once channeled, it is always used in some area that needs it.

Detachment is one of the prime requirements in healing work. "To let go, to open oneself as a channel for the healing flow, but to pray at the same time that the will of God should be done is the ideal—and to accept the inference of this prayer." We can sow seeds; we can open doors; but we cannot force those who are not ready for growth to go through the doors. Eventually their path will lead them to the same goal of Oneness, but some of them have a longer way to go, some a different way, and this we need to accept fully.

When there are strong emotional ties, it is difficult to be detached when healing; therefore it is probably better in these cases to ask for help from others who do not have the same emotional involvements with the one who is ill.

Feeling completely exhausted when working with people who need healing is an inevitable phase that most healers experience, unless they are able to bring through considerable experience from a past life. This is because the healer has become too involved personally, either consciously or unconsciously.

> It is not enough merely to be aware of the need to be personally uninvolved in the healing process; it requires considerable experience in order to be able to set the involvement aside at all levels. It is part of the process of learning to be a passive healing instrument.

As this feeling is usually experienced during the initial phases of learning to be a healer, we are advised not to attempt too much at the beginning. The need is great, and when we find that the healing forces can be channeled through us, there is often a temptation to do too much. We are told to resist this temptation and to increase our healing activity only as experience eliminates the feelings of exhaustion. This form of healing cannot be brought about consciously but only through prayer and complete surrender to being a channel for the healing energies. "The healing force is positive; where there is a real desire to heal others no serious or lasting harm will happen to any healer, however inexperienced." Nevertheless, it is advisable gradually to strengthen one's aura in order to protect oneself against negative vibrations.

An exercise that Gildas suggests we can practice in meditation is to imagine that our whole aura is being surrounded by a protective healing light. If we can produce the image strongly enough, such protection will occur. After any session of violent emotional expression by the patient, the healer should enclose the healing room or center in a band of light, and then pray, or in some way ask for the forces of light. Where our thought and our intent are pure and positive, we are assured that protection is automatically provided.

Certain symbols have great power if used correctly for protection and for requesting help from the spirit plane. They also have great power for healing. These symbols are a hexagon, any of the stars, various forms of the cross, the square, the circle and many others. We may discover our own symbol of healing power through meditation or intuition. When we know our symbol, in meditation or quiet thought, we can visualize it over the place that needs healing. If we concentrate well and send light to surround the symbol and shine forth from it, it will automatically bring help and power from "the other side."

Forgiveness

Gildas says that forgiveness is a very important factor, but it has to be complete forgiveness from the heart, which neither demands nor expects anything in return. This is a very difficult step to reach for human beings. Christ and the central figures in other faiths have all demonstrated this quality. Where this can be achieved, karmic debts are canceled out for the one who is forgiven and very much modified for the one who forgives. However, forgiveness of this type is very much a demand for perfection, and the true implications of what such forgiveness means will be understood only by a few.

Gildas suggests, therefore, that we start by *acceptance* as a step on the way to this total forgiveness. When we reach the stage where we can accept not only the pattern of others, but also our own pattern with all of its implications, on every level, then we are ready to forgive completely; but this acceptance must always come first. Acceptance of the whole pattern with its joy and its pain, and acceptance of the place in that pattern which each must fill, comes first. Then the total forgiveness and outflowing of love will follow soon afterwards almost as a natural stage of growth.

Forgiveness comes only with total understanding. When someone says, "I cannot forgive," we need to remember that this is only a small part of the total process. All of us are loved and forgiven by God even before we ask for these things.

> At the ego level there may be difficulties, self-punishments, exterior events seen as punishments, and the many mechanisms with which you are all too familiar. At a higher level these difficulties disappear.

Causes of Disease

Gildas says that orthodox medicine has paid much more attention in recent years to the interaction of mind and body and to psychosomatic disorders. Now we are urged to move a little further in our thinking so that the interaction, not only of mind and physical body, but of the spirit and the subtler bodies, will also be recognized and investigated.

The cause of the attacks on humanity by the new viruses is mainly that man has lost the ability to see himself as a whole being, including both physical and spiritual aspects. The business of healing has become quite chaotic when thought of in whole terms. "Only part of man is being healed most of the time and great areas are being laid open and vulnerable to attack by entities which will use any means to achieve a negative hold on man." These entities are the dark entities from the astral plane, which sometimes, where only partial healing has taken place, can gain a temporary but traumatic hold in the aura of the sick person and cause attacks that are interpreted as severe virus infections. On the mental level these attacks manifest as mental illness of varying degrees. "The art of exorcism, if rediscovered and revived, could free many of the mentally ill from the hospitals."

If we are sure that our diet and habits are temperate, Gildas suggests that we try to regard disease with a more positive attitude. We can seek help at such times through prayer, meditation and the various channels of healing. If our mind is sufficiently centered and quiet, we may begin to understand some of the reasons behind our illness.

> The reason may be one of many, ranging from karmic to a somewhat concrete form of conflict with the forces of darkness which are rendered considerably active in these difficult days preceeding the great planetary changes that are to come.

(Gildas covers these in some detail in the book *Gildas Communicates*, by the same authors.)

Gildas says that sickness and dis-ease are often necessary for positive growth; without them there could be no vision of perfection and completion; once we become conscious of a disease, then we can both give and accept healing, and harmonious progress is assured:

> There *is* some intrinsic value in the experience of pain; it is often part of the karma to be redeemed which was undertaken by the higher self before incarnation. The cause of the pain can also have direct reference to the karmic learning process.

> Cancer has several aspects and purposes. Firstly it is very much used on a karmic level, enabling some, through this suffering and experience, to redeem considerable karma in the course of one lifetime. Cancer is also part of a great mutational change in the form of matter, and it is necessary for this change to take place at levels of karmic suffering not only at the personal level, but at the greater world, group and racial levels. It is all part of the preparation for the New Age. Many great souls take to themselves this burden at some stage in their life.
>
> Cancer also at another level has presented an immense challenge, and the knowledge of the formation of the human physical cells which has been gained through research into cancer will be very much used in future healing. The treatments of cancer sometimes leave a great deal to be desired, but this is largely because of the lack of sensitivity

> to the human vehicle in its wider aspects, so that treatments are too strong, too drastic, too coarse. The ray treatments need much adjustment, but in principle they are similar to the specific use of very strong colors and light which is often given from this side where patients have cancer. In the future, when all the factors involved are recognized, cancer will be quite easily "curable," and will continue to appear, but in a more positive light as part of the necessary changes for the New Age pattern.

Death

Many people seek to prolong life by transplants because they are afraid of death. If only the basic truths could become more widely known, much further suffering would be prevented. There is so much human suffering involved in heart and liver transplants, and animal suffering involved in learning the skills necessary for these operations. It will all need to be redeemed at some future time. In healing we are asked to seek to alleviate suffering, to cure disease, not merely to prolong life, because we do not begin to understand life's purpose and its scope or the mysteries that lie beyond death:

> No man can be made to live longer than the span which has been ordained for him, for though the physical may appear to keep going, the spirit will depart when the time for its departure approaches, so that all the labor, all the clever techniques, all the suffering, are expended for a cause not worthy of the quality of these things.

Gildas says that the effects of transplant surgery upon the etheric bodies of both the person who receives a transplant and the person from whom the transplant is taken are serious and considerable.

> This is a branch of surgery which man would do well to give up. Life has its span, and it is time that the medical world begins to accept this. When a person dies, the etheric body draws from the physical body a certain essence which is used on the next plane of existence, and missing organs can cause certain disturbances to the period of transition from one state of being to the next.

On the other hand, euthanasia is never in accordance with the cosmic or karmic laws. Each person is allowed his span of life, and before incarnation the higher self of each individual accepts the lessons and sufferings for them. "The span should be lived naturally and normally, and ideally no interference should be made either to end it prematurely or to prolong it artificially."

Reincarnation

Gildas teaches that reincarnation is a valid fact, and that karma is the spiritual law of cause and effect running through consecutive incarnations; it is the reason for living many lives. He says:

> The path of physical incarnation and reincarnation is long and slow, some make it longer and slower than necessary; each path is different but leads eventually to the one goal. Any very difficult or trying life situation or relationship can usually be found to be karmic in origin. In all human experience, the karmic factor is inevitably present. The way in which one lives is all part of the karmic path, and all experience is either undertaken because of past life happenings, or is part of the path which will lead to future learning and knowledge.

The destiny of humanity is a continuous path towards Wholeness, Harmony, and Unity, and thus the individual becomes a whole self healed on every level. Every aspect of life is important as we travel along this path, and the influences and forces surrounding us on every level are all involved in the total picture. Thus the laws of karma are all part of the healing path, and in this way disharmony and disease may be regarded as contributing towards a final integral wholeness on every level of experience and being.

Karmic law does not deny man's free will; the soul will choose its own way. The higher self can only choose something of the life pattern and try to offer guidance.

> The Christian idea of redemption does fit into this pattern, since one's sins can be redeemed by the willingness to atone, and to follow an example and to live rightly. Those who endeavor to follow Christ automatically redeem their karma and are thus redeemed through Him.

The main lesson that karma teaches us today is tolerance. Humanity as a whole tends to be very intolerant. We must not judge; we do not know our own karma, let alone that of other people. In the interests of karma, some souls take on very difficult roles, but roles which are necessary for the final integration of all things.

Karma cannot be avoided by receiving healing, nor can it be worked off vicariously. Healing can give strength of purpose and body, or any other assistance necessary to the soul that wants to advance, but it cannot and will not lessen actual suffering if it is part of the karmic balance. Some conditions of karmic origin cannot be made to pass away during the current incarnation. Healers can never relieve suffering and illness that a person experiences as a result of heavy karma, unless it is the right time for some of that karma to be lifted, or unless a healing will result in a karmic lesson that is needed. If suffering or illness is karmic, healing can still be of value if the sufferer is helped to bear his trials more easily and more creatively, even though the pain is not removed. In addition, if the individual can realize the necessary understanding and achieve harmony throughout his being, then a particular karmic burden may be removed.

> If the patient is karmically ready for healing, the healer will be there. It may be on rare occasions that the higher self will have taken a decision before the present incarnation not to accept healing, though it may have been karmically earned at one particular point, but this decision will also have been made for karmic reasons, so the dividing line is very thin indeed.

We are told that the karmic path does not cease between lives and that the time spent on the other side is all part of the experience of the soul, but in a different dimension. When a soul is incarnated with an imperfect body, it is not due to a defective creation; the higher self may have deliberately chosen bodily imperfections for karmic purposes: "Sometimes an old soul, wishing to serve others and to hasten their spiritual development, may incarnate in a pitiful body in order to stimulate compassion."

Suffering

The learning process is often painful, but after the pain we will find that we are better equipped than before to work for the light and to help others. We will be tested and tried, sometimes tired and depressed, but always our guides and the light will be close to us, and all will eventually be well. Gildas comforts us with the thought that many experience the sort of feelings we have in those times. It is all part of the tension of the age. We must refuse to be drawn down into the negative and the dark.

> Many tasks are given to those upon the path. Often the task given to the individual may seem to

> be the hardest thing that could have been asked of him, while the task of another may seem to be more attractive; yet a great and wonderful pattern lies behind all things, and once the feet of the individual are upon the path, much will be asked of him, although much also may be given.

Gildas says that nothing is asked of us which we have not the strength to handle, and that help, healing, and encouragement are always available. We may be sure that all our helpers and guardians are nearby, and though our path may lead through some unpleasant experiences, we will be brought eventually safely through them and into a more normal sense of strength and consciousness again. We must be very patient. No suffering is undergone without reason or purpose of a higher order.

These are difficult times; the cosmic changes and unrest are affecting many individuals. We cannot avoid being bored and frustrated; we just have to live through it until the way ahead, the new direction, is very clear. We are urged not to make any movement until we *know* unavoidably that it is right, indeed *must be* because no other route presents itself. Times of waiting are always hard, but this is all part of the changing times.

The desolation of the soul is well known, but Gildas says there is no corresponding feeling in the spirit world among the more developed spirits:

> The rhythm of crucifixion and rising from the dead, of death and rebirth, are basic to the path of the human soul and have to be accepted as such. In the spirit world this rhythm is past, and the truth and joy of everlasting life is a vivid reality.

Gildas reminds us that the growth and the true birth of life takes place in the darkness of the earth, long before the actual blossoming in the spring. The true surge of energy and new life may not come until the spring, but that from which life is created often comes from out of the darkness.

8

AGARTHA

THIS BOOK contains valuable teaching on many aspects of spiritual life by a spirit entity who calls himself Mentor, and who gave these words to the author by thought transference during her times of meditation over a period of two and a half years (1981–83). In the book, Mentor's words are interwoven with her own description of what was happening, her feelings and thoughts in reaction to what he said, and her silent questions, which were always answered in subsequent sessions.

"Agartha" is the name given to the author by Mentor, who says it means "Journey to the Stars" and comes from a Sanskrit word, *agarta*, meaning "Heaven bound," which we all are. Mentor explains that this transference of ideas was possible because all beings on the physical and spiritual planes are integral and inseparable parts of the whole. The book includes some teaching on healing which has been selected and summarized as follows.

AGARTHA: A JOURNEY TO THE STARS, by Meredith Lady Young, is published by Stillpoint Publishing Company, P.O. Box 640, Meetinghouse Road, Walpole, NH 03608.

Healing

When we are ill or in pain, Mentor suggests that a solution can be found by talking to our own conscious mind as if we could see it. Ask it to bring into our consciousness any information which relates to our healing and contributes to a resolution of our problem. Within several days, answers and more questions will come into our awareness. He says:

> Disease, dysfunction or trauma of any kind is the clue that the need for some kind of change is at hand. If one repeatedly blocks change, the enmeshed negativity causes disease by its inability to be moved through one's presence thus stagnating the energies of one's system.

The pathway to health is one of change and the recognition of a need for change, but all too often people resist change. Yet the lessons of releasing the physical world in order to claim the cosmic are inevitably intense. Everyone needs to move through changes to find true peace. Fear of change is the only problem. When change is allowed to flow through our life in whatever way it will, without resistance, there is no fear or pain. It is ultimately the sick person who heals himself, but there can be no healing without effort on his part and the willingness to open himself to the possibility of change.

Mentor says that there are three stages in the trauma of a serious disease:

Stage 1. The patient needs a period of physical, psychological and spiritual seclusion in order to strengthen himself to transcend the disease which has resulted from unresolved changes. This conditions the mind and body to understand how he is off center. This is part of the healing process. Unfortunately friends and family misunderstand this withdrawal and try to terminate it. Most people blame their problems on "fate" instead of accepting them as signals of the need for change. This stage produces peace and ends with a sense of purposeful intent.

Stage 2. The patient identifies a direction to follow with trust. It is a transition between Stages 1 and 3.

Stage 3. A conscious decision to die or to live is sought and reached. It is the acceptance of the changes essential to physical and spiritual life that leads to life and healing. Sometimes the change required is lovingly to accept the situation without resentment.

Mentor teaches that visualization is unequaled in its effectiveness for adjusting the actual physical functioning of the body and washing away undesirable negative vibrations. Using visualization, "the conscious mind, and subsequently the conscious body, become aware of the potential perfect functioning of an organ and can then see what has to be changed to create that condition."

Mentor says that it is not possible to be healed without first gaining a new inner perspective. The understanding precedes, or is simultaneous with, any healing. Healing alters total reality and perfection is embraced. Healing through self-awareness is the only honest healing—one's view of reality changes.

The Healer

A healer is advised to uncover the cause of the disease to the best of his ability—physiologically, emotionally, and spiritually, and then lovingly to share this with the sick person so that the latter can choose, and take responsibility for, what action he will take. A true healer will never override a patient's wishes. It is important that we strive for balance in every aspect of our lives. Unless we recognize that our thoughts and actions affect our total being, we shall create imbalance and potential sickness. It has never been enough to treat the symptoms of an illness while ignoring the emotions, mind, and spirit of that person. The whole person must be considered and brought into balance.

If we think of ourselves as healers, giving and receiving love, we can feel reassured by the limitless power of love. Mentor says:

> All people are healers, and each is capable of healing not only his own presence, but his children, parents, close friends, distant relatives and total strangers. Every physical life situation has the potential for healing, for causing transformation. Life exists as a lesson in the art of healing oneself, each other, the planet and beyond. The purpose of physical life is to learn to heal.

Healing occurs through the creative process. Artists, musicians, teachers, business executives, lawyers, and others can all heal by creatively interpreting their profession.

When we choose to believe that we are powerless, we limit ourselves, and the energy is finite. If we believe that we are one with the Universe and allow ourselves to be infused with that limitless power, the energy becomes cosmic. Cosmic energy surrounds us; if we become aware of its existence, we can experience it and use it. All is possible if we trust in this. Mentor says:

> There is no limitation to what one's life can be on Planet Earth. Quite literally one creates every aspect of living. Personal power is manifested in the energy generated by conscious choice and is both finite and cosmic in nature.

This is real, not imaginary power; we need to believe in it and claim it for ourselves. The main generating source is God. Each individual can develop his connection with the Source and develop this limitless power. "Personal power is taking the energy of human endeavor and infusing it with the power of a universal or God-connection." We can use the power for ourselves, which is an abuse of power, or give it away to another and thus become obliged to follow another's path, or we can increase it by using it for higher spiritual purposes. We can gain this power either by seeking a known goal, or by searching for an unknown meaningful direction.

Of interest to those who participate in a healing circle or group is that Mentor confirms what modern physicists have been saying, namely that the energy or power of a group with a common vision increases in proportion to the number of people in the group *squared.* This means that 20 people in a unified group equals 400 units of viable energy, and 15,000 persons in the USA with a unified vision would have the equivalent potential power of the total U.S. population without a unified vision. 64,000 people with one mind could change the planet!

Love

The universal energy of Divine Love is the force that heightens another's vibrations, dissolves their negativity, and reforms their being into unity. However:

> The individual's willingness to accept love into their life will, to a large degree, effect the healing. For in being healed, one actually changes vibrational rates, overriding the established level of energy within the body. The new energy causes an intensive cleansing within the body which frees the physical body from its load of aquired negativity and confusion.

In other words, the healer adds sufficient energy to the other person's whole being so that their body reestablishes its own unique balance. Mentor says that it is necessary to visualize a direct link-up of the positive love energy with the negative disease energy, so that the former can transmute the latter.

Mentor says that

> Love is the vibration which when expanded through cosmic attunement produces "miracles." It is un-

> limited. Love given with no sense of self-glorification or personal achievement, is the thread woven through every healing. Love is experienced by all realities.

On Mentor's plane it is "an expression beyond individual limitation." On the earth plane

> there is little concern for love as universal harmony, because there is only a budding understanding of man's connection to the whole; and physical awareness through development of human relationships is the most important exercise of life, with a new growing concern for individual spiritual advancement. As love is seen in its true proportions, so involvement in, and concern for, the universal growth and advancement of all energies becomes the living focus of all.

Causes of Disease

Mentor points out that there are both negative and positive energies or vibrations, and that the negative ones can create disease. This can grow from a minor ailment to a chronic illness as the negativity attracts more negative vibrations, possibly increasing to a terminal illness if the circuit is not broken. He mentions food as an example of an energy which can be either negative or positive; so can the thoughts and actions of others. Whether these vibrations are processed as positive or negative depends on the interpretation or outlook of the receiver as well as the sender.

Waves of positive energy passing through a physical body heal, cleanse, and attune by aligning all the bodily energies. They do their work, then pass out of the body. Negative energy becomes caught within the body's fibers and causes imbalance. When mental, emotional, physical, and spiritual vibrations are misaligned, the degree of disease that results is in direct proportion to the amount of disharmony.

Mentor describes stress, which is now generally accepted by orthodox medicine as a cause of disease, as the "acceptance of overwhelming negative energy into one's body without the counterbalance of cleansing." He maintains that it contributes to many diseases of mind and body, not just heart attacks, and also results in the aging process. He says that children who are born with physical or mental deficiencies have not totally developed their sense of self. They are still more strongly connected to the nonphysical vibration of the spirit life than to the physical vibration of the Earth plane. Great care should be taken with such children to help them develop a sense of self in the physical world through touch, sound, color, and gentle manipulation.

Death

Our life in a physical body, whether it is a few months or a hundred years, is but a moment of eternity. We learn from life on earth in two ways: "Functionally" by living in the body and "Observationally" by looking at physical-life experience from the wider viewpoint of life on the spirit plane. Death, therefore, does not stop the learning process for spiritual growth. Mentor says that "death is not an end to viable expression but a change in vibration. Vibration is the common denominator of all forms of life. It is also the means of identifying individual life forms." That is, each form of life, whether plant, animal, or human, has its own unique vibrational pattern. Each individual life is special and important for the harmony of all life.

It is fruitless for us to try to judge why an individual dies, because there is a correct time for that individual to live and a correct time for them to die, each one in accordance with their choice. It depends on the total cosmic journey of the individual soul or higher consciousness.

If at the time of impending death we consciously release the physical life instead of resisting its loss, the nonphysical vibration, which is always present, becomes dominant and there is no experience of pain regardless of the cause of death. Here again, resistance creates pain. In the case of a lingering illness, if the dying person will consciously and without fear allow the nonphysical vibration to increase and the physical vibration to decrease, the pain, if any, will be minimized.

Reincarnation

Mentor not only treats reincarnation as a fact of Life but says that we are living many lifetimes simultaneously (a concept also taught by Seth) and that "it is impossible to accurately assess a singular lifetime without seeing it in relation to the whole or composite of many simultaneously existing lifetimes." Each of us in fact is many characters at the same time.

Each time we are given a new body it gives us the freedom to create something fresh. We need to recognize our heart's promptings as to the appropriate physical experience. Daring to follow the path of the heart ensures ultimate success. Mentor says:

> Considering the slow progress toward awareness, and the fact that most people do indeed die short of enlightenment, it becomes obvious that to achieve even relative cosmic understanding, the soul body needs more than a mere eighty years on earth.

If we have areas of change that were not resolved in a previous life, they will continue to appear in subsequent lives until the change is made. If an individual can actualize his healing of a disease caused by karma, then it will no longer need to reappear. Karma provides the opportunity for change—the outcome is determined by the choices that only the individual can make. If we choose the all-powerful vibration of love, we can overcome any karmic limitation. Mentor says:

> Disease, imbalance or any lack of wholeness, even though it springs to life through karma, cannot

> stand in the aura of love without being transmuted. In seeking healing one needs to realize that the complete acceptance of love into one's presence as the transformative experience is more powerful than any karmic reaction.

Once we have opened our eyes to our own unity with God and brought in that power, we are beyond the reach of karma, as long as we live in and by the Law of Love.

Mentor says that it is important to allow children relatively free rein in their early years when it comes to periods of sleep. Some need more periods of attunement and learning in the spirit planes than others do. They know intuitively what is needed to become well grounded. If deprived of this, they may decide to return to that plane. The amount of sleep that a child requires is a clue to its commitment to the Earth. The less the sleep required, the greater the commitment.

9

WHITE EAGLE

WHITE EAGLE is a spirit teacher who has lived on this planet as an American Indian Chieftain, a Tibetan, an Egyptian Priest-Pharaoh, and in many other situations. He has spoken through a medium, Mrs. Grace Cooke, for over 40 years, teaching spiritual truths that have been published by the White Eagle Publishing Trust in a number of books. Three of these, listed in the footnote, are consulted here for their teachings on healing.

In the first of these texts, White Eagle gives his interpretation of the Gospel of John. It is well known that this gospel contains much information on the healings performed by Jesus and his teaching about that activity. It seems possible, however, that from White Eagle's vantage point in the spirit world he can give us additional information, since he would not be affected by any omissions or errors resulting from the original delay in recording the

THE LIVING WORD OF SAINT JOHN and HEAL THYSELF, by White Eagle, and HEALING BY THE SPIRIT, by Ivan Cooke, are published by The White Eagle Publishing Trust, New Lands, Brewells Lane, Liss, GU33 7H9, Hampshire, England.

events and teaching, and from the many translations and revisions made since then.

Healing by the Spirit, written by Ivan Cooke, is full of literal quotations from White Eagle, and these have been studied for additional information on healing. The third book is a small one spoken by White Eagle specifically on this subject. Following is a synthesis of the teaching on healing extracted from these three books.

Healing

White Eagle says that

> All life's experiences have but one object, to raise the whole being of man from mortality to immortality. . . . your own part in becoming whole and healthy is to forget your symptoms and to concentrate instead on the Source of all life and light. Set your heart resolutely on the things of God. . . . Spiritual Healing is brought about by the power of spiritual aspiration; when the thoughts are truly aspiring, then the light of Christ, the rays of Christ, fall into the heart. . . . Light takes possession, dominating the body and controlling the physical atoms. This is how miracles are performed.

There is an invisible power that will heal, but we have to prepare our body, mind, and soul to allow this divine healing to flow in. We are spirit, and we are just as responsible for our own healing as any healer who tries to help us. Divine law requires the soul's cooperation for a complete healing. The lesson that the sickness was designed to teach must first be learned; so we are urged to pray to understand its cause and purpose.

If we will seek the presence of Christ, we shall receive perfect healing, because man is divine as well as human. Jesus was a man but he was irradiated by the Christ. A positive loving attitude towards life and people helps us to see their divine essence, and this starts the divine magic that heals.

Happiness is essential to good health, and inner happiness comes from knowing God. A happy soul does not die of disease, because every cell is under the control of God.

The Healer

White Eagle has the following advice for those who wish to heal others: The first step is self-purification. Next are love, tranquility, willingness to serve, and a strong willpower to concentrate the healing rays. All of these are necessary. Healers are also to preserve silence during the healing because it creates and preserves the healing power. White Eagle says, "Don't concentrate too much on physical symptoms . . . for you are dealing primarily with the patient's soul and aura. . . . Don't work too hard *of yourself*." Our job is to contact higher beings and to be a bridge for the spiritual forces. We are asked to picture the patient as perfect and concentrate on the spiritual aspect.

Healers are told to be unmoved by failure or success. The right attitude towards the work of healing is "Here am I, Lord, use me if you will, and may the healing of souls be to your honor and glory." Humility is essential. First comes our love for God, then love for our neighbor *and* for oneself. We are advised never to judge or condemn, but always to be gentle and loving. White Eagle says that the spiritual quality of the healer is supremely important, but he also emphasizes the importance of pure food and water, fresh air, sunlight, and pure thoughts for all healers; also, the value of deep breathing: "Breathe in the Holy Breath and Spiritual Life, and exhale blessings to all life."

When healing, we are to think of receiving the cosmic rays and letting them pour through our hands. However:

> Healing depends not so much on the laying-on of hands, but on a clear and full contact with Christ;

> the essence of Christ can then pour forth from the whole aura and can be intensified in its actions by the healer's mental control. This is the true healing.

Jesus said, "The Father and I are one." White Eagle says that this is the source of healing power. If we walk closely with God, the healing power will pour from us. Of ourselves we can do nothing; it is the power that works through us that accomplishes the will of God when we surrender ourselves to it. The perfect healer is one who acts only in accordance with that will.

Forgiveness

If anyone retains a desire for revenge against someone who has harmed him, he will remain chained to the other through the ages as the karmic debt bounces backwards and forwards between them. The only way to break this chain is for one of them to forgive the other. Jesus did this for Judas who betrayed him and for the soldiers who crucified him. "There must be forgiveness because without it the soul cannot be redeemed. It is a cosmic law which no soul can escape."

Love

White Eagle says that God's love for us is completely beyond our comprehension and that it will never fail us if we rely on it. It will sustain us through every ordeal that we are called upon to face. The greatest thing in life is love. If we serve others and share with others, with love from our hearts, and acknowledge the dignity of every living human or animal, we will find the way to cosmic consciousness. "The object of all spiritual striving, the answer to all problems, fears and pain, and the strong victor over death, is love." It is the greatest power in this world or the next and is inseparable from wisdom and power.

If we apply love, it will never fail, regardless of how difficult the problem may be. "Jesus healed through his outpouring of love—love was the key, love was the secret, but such a love as is rarely experienced or understood by men on earth." The Christ in Jesus was so completely at-one with the Father that the life force came to him without any obstruction. He could give that love to all he met and raise the vibration of each person so that they could respond to Divine Love.

When our consciousness is expanded, we shall recognize that love needs to be in every act and thought of our lives. When the Holy Spirit comes, we are reborn and the power of love flows through us and brings gifts of healing and the power to illumine others. If we pray only for what we can share, with no selfish motives, we are certain to receive an answer, because such prayer makes us a channel for Divine Love, and we know the answer.

"Love is the supreme power in the Universe. God is Love, and only when love is withdrawn from any situation can conflict and death ensue." We can only receive love if we give love. If the law of love is broken, suffering, disease, and pain will follow. If we can respond in absolute purity to the love of God, we will experience a sudden, complete, and true spiritual healing. However, White Eagle says that "such a deep healing is rare indeed, for few are ready to make so complete a surrender to the Love of God." Love *is* the law and when we put the law into operation, everything works for good in our lives. When we love, we are in direct contact with the Christ spirit. Eventually each one of us has to surrender to the Divine Law of Love, which rules throughout the universe. If we will train ourselves to think in terms of love and forgiveness in every moment of our lives, we shall experience a most beautiful healing.

Causes of Disease

White Eagle says that some disease is caused by violating our body, which is a temple of God. We are advised not to overtire or abuse it, deny it the right to food, or take it into danger. If we do, we are breaking a spiritual law. God created our body and we ought to respect it and love it; it is a vehicle that Christ can use in the service of all creation; it is not something from which to escape. Other diseases are caused by our thoughts of fear, anger, depression, or anxiety. These cut us off from the Source of Life and will manifest as disharmony in our psyche or body. Our minds, especially our subconscious minds, are full of fear, including the fear of death. Despondent minds invite an accident or misfortune, so we must practice positive and hopeful thinking.

Disease can also be caused by overstimulation of our mind or lack of control of our desires. The latter releases desires that are eventually reflected as disease and lack of harmony in mind or body. When man gives way to low emotions such as resentment, selfishness, greed, and hatred, he becomes controlled by his lower self, and his higher self is driven out. The power of Christ in man can overcome this weakness of the lower self and make man perfect.

Anything consistently inharmonious in a life may predispose the body to illness. Sickness of the body is the result of dis-ease in the soul, and it is through the soul body that healing of the physical body takes place:

> The fundamental cause of all the manifold diseases of man is a lack of spiritual light in the life of man; and the one true cure is the incoming of the Light of God into his life. . . . Jesus healed by pouring in the Light, pouring in spiritual rays which awaken the soul. . . . Continually to know God is to know health. . . . As man lives in spirit

> and by the Spirit of God, so he will create a more perfect physical body. This is a law.

If we are sick, we need to realize that our fear of the sickness will make it grow. Instead we are advised to concentrate on loving, kind, tolerant, and generous thoughts, and thoughts of God. "All sickness and accidents are manifestions of the failure of the physical cells to remain attuned to God."

He mentions one other cause of disease as being unrecognized, namely obsession or attachment by dark forces because in a past life the individual performed ill deeds and this karma returned when the soul reincarnated. These attachments work through the psyche to the physical body and manifest as disease or an accident. "Once the Divine Law of Life is understood it is seen that all things originate from a cause which lies deeper than mere carelessness or ignorance." If only psychologists and physicians could recognize the laws of reincarnation and karma, they would see that many conditions are due not only to subconscious memories harbored by the physical body, but also to soul memories.

Few of us realize that our material and physical problems are the outer expression of our inner life. For example, it is impossible to cure cancer purely by surgery, but it is not incurable. It is primarily a spiritual disease brought about by the breaking of natural and spiritual laws, not necessarily in the present life. This creates a block in the intake of the life essence. The patient's response to treatment will be in accordance with his state of spiritual evolution. The growing incidence of cancer is due to the increasing artificiality of the life man is forced to lead.

Our habitual thoughts either create or destroy. Inharmonious thoughts create disease. Harmonious thoughts bring health. If we think negative thoughts, we give them life. Stop thinking them, and we withdraw life from them and they gradually die. Good thoughts will not only build man's spiritual body but also his physical body. What we think today we become tomorrow; daily we re-create our body.

Death

It may not always be right for a physical healing to take place. Sometimes through the suffering and death of the body, indescribable good comes to the soul. We are not loving when we resent the release of a soul from bondage and darkness into light by so-called death. Rather we are told to rejoice and love, forgetting all selfish desires, longing, and pain. Those who have "died" are the same as when we formerly knew and loved them, but they are much happier because they are freed from the cares, distress, and confusion of earth. We are told to think of them as living more abundantly in a place we know they would love. When we pray for them and think about them, it opens the way for them to return. Their joy increases when they feel that we are attuned to them in our souls and believe and know that they are close.

White Eagle further says that we do not necessarily have to die before we too can pass freely into the spirit world and clearly see the life of those who live there. Communication between the so-called living and the so-called dead is always available to those who can develop within themselves a consciousness of the Oneness of all life.

Reincarnation

As with nearly all teachers from the Spirit Plane, reincarnation is taken for granted by White Eagle. He says:

> It is shown again and again in the gospel that the truths of reincarnation and karma were known by Jesus; indeed without knowledge of reincarnation we cannot fully understand the meaning underlying his teachings.

Innocent suffering does not exist. As onlookers, we do not know the past or future of the path followed by the sufferer, and so we are ignorant of the spiritual laws at work. Karma, which results from a man's negative or evil action, may result in material, emotional, or physical suffering along the way. If an "incurable" disease appears, it means that a final physical climax of experience is eliminating a weakness in that soul.

No one can run away from the lessons that life brings him. Every time he tries, he will be faced with the same cycle of experiences until the lesson has been learned. When someone asked Jesus to heal them, he could always see their karma, both good and bad, which their soul had collected. He also knew what their future would be because of what had happened in their past. When he healed them, the cure may have lasted only for that lifetime if the person's soul failed to respond, and it would have been confronted by that lesson in subsequent lives. But if that person responded to Divine Love, the healing would have been for eternity; for the karma would have been transmuted.

> Always karma can be transmuted through the redeeming power of God's love working in man. . . . The Christ within you can transmute your karma; in fact there is nothing it cannot accomplish. . . . When the soul fully realizes his at-one-ment with the divine life and allies himself with the Christ, then he is healed; made perfect.

White Eagle suggests that those who are physically blind or have defective vision may have been blinded by a spiritual light that has awakened their psyche. They may have come to the last step on their path of cleansing and development. However, we must be careful not to judge that the cause of someone's suffering is due to karma. There may be some other reason.

Whenever a complete cure of a so-called incurable disease takes place, it is because the sufferer has expiated his karma. Life is governed by the law of karma, but ultimately this law brings great happiness to everyone.

Suffering

White Eagle says that our troubles, accidents, and tragedies are a part of the natural process of soul development. What appears to us to be disaster will in the end be recognized by us as all part of a wonderful pattern of our soul's growth toward happiness and light. We are asked to try to be patient when we suffer, and to try to accept the experiences of our life without resentment, for resentment will only prolong the lesson. If we can accept all that happens to us as the operation of the Divine Law of Love, then we will rapidly pass through the lower planes of consciousness of earth's suffering into light and happiness. These experiences are not sent to us by God, but are a discipline resulting from the law of cause and effect, for we ourselves have at some time and place sown the seed. God does not inflict suffering, but He uses the suffering that man creates for himself to bring good into the individual life.

Sometimes a soul returning to earth may accept afflictions or sufferings in order to demonstrate a lesson to humanity as a service to God. For all of us, however,

> The story of the Christ birth and life, crucifixion, resurrection, and ascension, is a symbolic presentation of the life of every man. Every event in the ordered life-story of Jesus of Nazareth is an initiation which will happen in each human life.

When we see bodily or mental suffering in those we love, we are asked to remember that they are working through a condition of life that will eventually bring their soul into the light. "Hold them in the Light." Every soul seems to suffer, but, seen in its right perspective, it brings a rebirth.

10

SILVER BIRCH

FOR SIXTY-ONE YEARS Maurice Barbanell, who died in 1981, acted as a medium for the teachings of Silver Birch. Since 1938, much of this instruction has been published in books. *Light from Silver Birch* was the last of these.

When asked to identify himself, the spirit entity said:

> Silver Birch is not my name. It is the name of the Indian spirit I use as a transformer that enables me to lower my vibrations and reach your world. The name does not matter. I am not a red Indian. I belong to another race in another part of the world that goes back much further. I was asked to act as a messenger for some evolved spiritual beings—masters, if you like. I agreed to do so. I am not an infallible spirit teacher who never makes mistakes.

LIGHT FROM SILVER BIRCH, by Maurice Barbanell, is published by Psychic Press Ltd., 20 Earlham Street, London, WC2, England.

> The great value of what we have to offer is a sublime truth from the storehouse of Divine wisdom.

This book contains valuable teaching on many aspects of spirituality, with some of it devoted to healing.

Healing

God is All There Is, and a portion of God, whom Silver Birch calls the Great White Spirit, is within everybody and everything that lives. Nothing can ever sever that link, and because of it we have access to infinite wisdom. The power of love directs the plan of God, and we can each be the instruments of that power that streams from God and enables the sick to be healed. Our task is to become better instruments.

Silver Birch says that healing the soul is more important than healing the body, so that "the result will be increased awareness and understanding of eternal spiritual realities." If this is not done, the healing is a failure. It means that the sick person has been given the opportunity for spiritual growth and has not taken it. The physical body, mind, and spirit are three indivisible and essential parts of the one whole self. If we touch the soul, we help body and mind to achieve the wholeness that brings health. Disease indicates some blockage causing these parts of the whole to be out of balance and working inefficiently. "The most important thing is to help the sick ones realise they are spirits with bodies and the real individual is the deathless spirit."

Silver Birch reminds us that God is Love, and Love is the greatest power of all; it is the power of Spirit in operation.

> Healing is from the Great Spirit, by the way of the healer's spirit, to the patient's spirit. The power of the Spirit, which emanates from its Divine Source, is transmitted to a healer who has the gift of heal-

> ing, which is a spiritual one. Through him the power is directed to the spirit of the sufferer. The whole exercise is a spiritual one. The spirit, being the life force, will try to produce harmony where there was disharmony.

Some people are ready to be healed spiritually, and so are healed; others are not ready spiritually, and so are not healed.

The Healer

When we agree to serve, we shall be guided. The task of healing is not easy, but power will always be provided to overcome any difficulty. As we become more receptive, we shall be able to receive greater knowledge, and as we develop, more spirit power will flow through us. However, things of the spirit cannot be hastened beyond their natural growth—it is a slow steady process, one step at a time. Love is stronger than death. Life and Love are powers of God which we all possess and can use as we develop them to serve others. We will be shown the way when we are spiritually ready to receive direction.

"Spiritual healing uses a divine power which emanates from the Supreme Creator. Its quality, quantity and nature depend on the development of the healer as to the amount and type that can be registered through him or her." Everyone who seeks to grow will experience loneliness, but evolved beings will always help and give strength and inspiration. Silver Birch says that there are higher, evolved beings in spirit whose one desire is to help, inspire, and utilize us as channels for the Divine power that can heal the sick and guide those who wish to progress. As healers, we must be available and never refuse help when it is sought. We are asked to do the best we can. What the other person does afterward is his or her responsibility. We cannot heal everyone who comes. Some are not ready; others must endure their disease for karmic reasons. We are urged to give credit for healings to God and not to take the responsibility for failure. Silver Birch is opposed to transplanting any part of the human body to another person.

Causes of Disease

Many people today live in an unbalanced environment under stressful conditions, and this creates an increasing amount of disease. Physical disease in most cases is the outward manifestation of an inner disharmony.

Death

Inevitably there is sadness when someone we love dies. But it is only a physical separation, not a spiritual one. Death cannot separate those whom love has joined. We shall survive death because we have no alternative; surviving is part of the natural law—it is automatic. Our spirit comes to earth to develop, grow, and prepare itself for its real home where we began. Death is a door which opens to reveal the wondrous life of the realms of the spirit. "Death is the great liberator; death brings freedom. . . . The individual is ready to enjoy all the tremendous richness and beauty that the spirit life has to offer."

Reincarnation

Silver Birch talks freely of reincarnation as a fact with many facets.

> It is part of the law of cause and effect in operation because there are karmic debts to be paid. If a patient has a karmic condition carried over from a previous life and the karma is not complete, the healing will appear to fail. If the patient is spiritually developed to where the effect has completely

> followed the cause and there is no more karma to manifest, the healing will be successful because the soul is ready.

We choose our path before we return to this plane, but we can rest assured that justice is a natural law and will always prevail.

Suffering

The one area that Silver Birch differs from most of the other spirit teachers is his emphasis on the necessity for all those who are healers, or on the spiritual path, to suffer. He says:

> It is not possible to achieve even the first steps in spiritual mastery unless you are ready to do so by a process which means that you must suffer. Suffering is the crucible. Those on whom the Great Spirit, with infinite wisdom, has bestowed the gift of healing must experience difficulty, sorrow, crisis and trial so that they can have compassion for the ones who will come to them in their suffering and ask for healing. . . . Spiritual growth is not achieved when the sun is shining and the sky is cloudless, but it is when all looks dark, gloomy and depressing.
>
> We have latent qualities which can only be manifested when confronted with difficulty, adversity and obstacles. There has to be heartbreak, sorrow, and suffering to appreciate fully the compensations that will follow. Those who will serve must be tried and tested, sometimes to their uttermost strength.

However, there is a law of compensation that operates automatically, and the healer is rewarded by serving others as he was served and shown the way. The burden is never heavier than can be borne. If we live in harmony with the natural laws, we will find an inner peace and resolve that will ensure success.

We have to endure privation, perhaps ill health, or some crisis that will touch our soul. Silver Birch says that there is no other way. The soul will awaken in the depths of despair and emerge with a greater expression of divinity.

11

SYNTHESIS

EXAMINING ALL of these teachings on healing, we find a great deal of agreement on the fundamentals, and special emphasis on certain features. This chapter endeavors to synthesize the teachings and extract the essence from the total.

Love

It seems clear that the key element in Cosmic Healing is Love. God is Love. We were created by Love, and we are sustained and healed by Love. Love is what we are; this is our identity. Pure Love is unconditional. This means that there are no conditions, expectations, or possessive aspects to it. In channeling this Love for healing, a response is not a requirement. In fact, the response could be anger or otherwise negative without affecting the flow of Love from and through the one desiring to serve another.

This Love is the only power in the world, and it is within every one of us, ready to be used. Nothing can withstand it. Love is the center of the whole universe, and from this center a continuous flow of Love flows through every soul and everything that lives. It cannot be withheld from anyone. When we are loving, we surround that which we are loving with the Radiant Presence and Activity of God.

When we look away from Love we are deliberately and consciously choosing the experience of chaos, which will inevitably follow. It is the One Law of Life, the action principle of God. We cannot exist without it. Only when love is withdrawn from any situation can conflict and death ensue. The enormity of God's love for us is completely beyond our comprehension because there is nothing on earth with which it can compare, but it will never fail us if we rely on it.

God loves everyone equally because we are all part of God. Love is complete in itself and so asks for nothing in return. We can always receive this wonderful gift of Love that is being poured out eternally. We can experience It for ourselves by opening ourselves up to It. It is eagerly waiting to express Itself from the very center of our being.

When attempting to heal another, we are advised to work with the energy of Divine Love. We are to will the Love of God to flow through ourselves, thinking the word LOVE and feeling the love as it flows. Jesus healed by his outpouring of love, which raised the vibrations of each person so that they could respond to Divine Love. Love is an indispensable element in healing, as it is the fundamental principle upon which all Perfection rests. If we use it without limitation, nothing will be impossible to us; however, the individual's willingness to accept the love into his or her life enables the healing to be effective.

Self-healing is entirely possible if we make a *complete* surrender to the Love of God, in which case we shall experience a sudden and complete healing. However, few of us are willing to do this. If we wish to attain this point, we must train ourselves to think in terms of love and forgiveness in every moment of our lives, constantly filling our thoughts and feelings with Divine Love, and remembering that we can only receive love if we give love. Love increases as it is given.

There is really nothing new in this teaching. Nearly two thousand years ago, when Jesus was asked which was the greatest commandment, he said:

> You shall love the Lord your God with all your heart, and with all your soul, and with all your mind. . . . And a second is like it, you shall love your neighbor as yourself. On these two commandments depend all the law and the prophets. (Matt. 22:37–40).

Why did he say the second is like the first? Because our neighbor is a part of God—God is All There Is. So, when we love other humans, we are loving God. Jesus lived what he preached, loving all men, women, and children unconditionally, and proving it in countless ways. Finally, shortly before his death, he said, "A new commandment I give to you that you love one another; even as I have loved you" (John 13:34). Very soon after saying this he demonstrated how great his love was by forgiving the soldiers who were driving the nails into his hands.

We are told that Divine Love consciously directed to accomplish things produces marvelous results. If we use it without limit, nothing will be impossible to us, and it will be perfect protection against anything that might harm us. One example of the infinite power of Love was told to me by a man who had experienced pain and suffering for forty-five years. He had tried various methods of healing, both orthodox and unorthodox, but nothing had helped. One day after several long, prayerful meditations asking for Divine Guidance, he became aware of the biblical emphasis on Love and its infinite power. He was then guided to focus his mind totally on the word Love to the exclusion of all other thoughts, including his pain and suffering.

It took him about two hours to achieve this state, and then he realized that the pain was beginning to dissolve and healing was taking place. From then on he did his utmost to stay focused on Love at all times and in all situations.

To the extent that he is able to do this he has remained free of pain and free of stress and fear.

Forgiveness

Another important element in Cosmic Healing is forgiveness, which in fact has to precede Love if the love is to be unconditional. "Forgiveness is the source of healing . . . the only road that leads out of disaster, past all suffering and finally away from death." In fact, "All problems are caused by unforgiveness" (*A Course in Miracles*). The way that we can become fully aware that we are all One, all part of God, is to forgive; this destroys the illusion of separateness and brings the realization that therefore there is nothing to forgive. Real forgiveness heals the forgiver and the forgiven. It is essential that the forgiveness itself be unconditional and from the heart. "In the heart is the meeting place of God and man; you can meet Him face to face when you have forgiven all" (*Divine Healing of Mind and Body*).

In comparing the teachings that came through these ten different channels, we find that the emphasis varies here and there, but they are largely very consistent. However, there is an interesting contradiction between two of the teachings on the question of God's forgiveness. *A Course in Miracles* says that we do not need to ask God for forgiveness because He never condemned us—all we need to do is to accept His Love, which is completely unconditional, and we know that we are forgiven. On the other hand, the lectures in Chapter 2 (*Divine Healing of Mind and Body*) say that God forgives us the moment we ask for forgiveness because He loves us. He forgives us when we forgive others their faults, but if we do not forgive in our own hearts, there can be no forgiveness. This condition is not mentioned in any of the other teachings, but it is in the New Testament: "If you do not forgive men their trespasses, neither will your Father forgive your trespasses" (Matt. 6:15).

Saint Germain says that we shall experience complete freedom if we pour out Unconditional and Eternal forgiveness to everybody and everything. But unless the discord is forgotten, it is not forgiven; we cannot release ourselves from the discord until it is out of our consciousness.

Forgiveness has to come before healing can be permanent. Since complete forgiveness is very difficult for many people, an intermediate step is to accept the other's behavior, as well as our own. When that has been accomplished, total forgiveness becomes possible. Retaining a desire for revenge against someone who has harmed us chains us to the other person through the ages. The only way to break this is by forgiveness.

Thoughts, Feelings, and Beliefs

The third factor in Cosmic Healing that is emphasized by these teachings is that we create all of our physical experiences in life, including disease and pain, by our thoughts, feelings, and beliefs, and therefore we can heal these problems by choosing to think and feel differently. Our thoughts are exclusively our own. We have a free will and therefore have control over our thoughts—no one else does. Thus we have the power to change them and, as a result, change our experience of disease into one of health. We cannot change the symptoms or the disease itself, only the thoughts behind them. We decide what we believe; if we believe we are well, that will be our experience.

Our body cannot create pain or disease by itself, but our thoughts and feelings can. In effect, we choose to be ill and even choose the kind of illness. Seth says that we can obtain a clear picture of what is going on within us by looking at what is happening outside us. What seems to be an objective, concrete event, independent from ourselves, is actually the materialization of our inner emotions, energy, and thoughts. Thus our conscious thoughts and feelings regulate our health. There are no idle thoughts; they all produce results in some form at some level. The mind creates and action follows. It is essential that the one who desires to be healed take responsibility for his life and for the changes that are necessary. He cannot simply do nothing and wait for someone else, or God, to heal him.

Many of the teachings emphasize the Perfection of God and that, as the creations or children of God, we too are perfect. If we allow God to control our lives, then we will experience that perfection in our bodies and minds. Anything else is an illusion. We need to embrace the Perfection that is. The teachings also talk of the importance of recognizing the Christ or the God-Self within ourselves and every other person. This is God manifesting Himself and urging man to awaken to his eternal Divine Consciousness. God is within everybody, and within man lie all the powers of God. The Christ of God is the living Presence of God in each and every one of us. If we awaken to that fact, all power will manifest itself through us. There is but one Source of Life and that is the God-Self within every individual. It is the Supreme Power of all creation and is limitless. That which is external is of no value.

Several teachers describe the power of visualization (a combination of thought, feeling, and imagination) both in the creation of the illusion of disease and in the healing process.

Prayer

The importance of prayer in healing and as a part of life in general is mentioned in several places. *A Course in Miracles* says that the only meaningful prayer is for forgiveness, because those who have been forgiven have everything. In another place it says that the only prayer that is necessary is to repeat God's name and then everything will fall into right perspective. The words used in prayer are unimportant; God understands what comes from the heart. The really sacred place is within our own heart, and there we can speak to God. Only there in the silence of love, with all physical senses stilled, can our prayers be truly heard. It is important to believe that we have received that for which we have asked; then we will have it.

Jesus says, "Prayer is the breathing of the breath of life. It is the most powerful thing in all planes and in all worlds. Live in the thought of Love towards all, and your life will become one continuous prayer" (*Divine Healing of Mind and Body*). He also says that the most efficient prayer that we can offer to God is helpfulness to those in need of help. God never fails to notice any prayer, and He blesses all our efforts. The answer may not appear completely right away, but we are urged not to be discouraged. If we ask firmly, we shall receive.

Being a Healer

We are told that anyone can be a channel for healing if they offer themselves for this purpose and keep their own will out of the way. God has given all of His gifts freely and equally to everyone—He has no favorites. The positive, conscious desire to be of service is the most important factor; however, this has to be coupled with relaxed receptivity, avoiding an intense desire to heal. We are to heal out of our love for God and our desire to serve Him according to His will, and without any conscious desire to choose the nature of our service. The time, the place, and the nature of the service will be provided by unseen forces. Service to another is actually service to God, because the other is in truth His Substance. Every effort to serve accumulates experience until Cosmic Healing is demonstrated.

If we wish to heal, the wish has to come from the heart and not from the ego or a sense of duty. We are urged to surrender to God every aspect of human existence—physical, mental, and spiritual—and every desire. Above all, we are told to surrender our own will, which is the chief lesson we came to learn on the earth plane. We are also to surrender the desire to heal or the desire to see the other person get well. If the surrender is really complete, we shall experience Cosmic Consciousness and Cosmic Power, and we shall become an open channel to be used as God wills. Healing cannot be accomplished by a conscious effort or a will to heal—only by surrender. When a healing does occur, we are not to rejoice at being instrumental in the healing, but rather we are to give the glory to God.

Healing is an ability everyone can develop, and needs to develop, if he is to be healed. If we think that we have some ability that others do not have, we do not understand God. If we are concerned with results, we will limit the healing and demonstrate doubt and lack of trust. Continued concern appears to be a demonstration of love, but love without trust is impossible. Underneath the doubt about results is self-doubt—a concern with the self, not the patient. Detachment is a prime requirement for a healer, seeking only that the will of God be done, and being unmoved by failure or success.

We are told always to hold the thought that God never fails and that it is He who is doing the work in accordance with His will. Whenever anyone is willing to be a channel for healing, there are evolved beings on the Spirit plane who are willing and eager to help when asked to do so. However, it is up to us to ask, because they will never impose their will upon ours.

In order to heal others successfully, it is essential for the healer to allow all his own mistakes to be gradually corrected. God will show him how to do this if He is asked. In helping others, it is far better to help them to understand the underlying mental, emotional, or spiritual cause of their problem, and then to show them how to help themselves through the creative power of the Christ that dwells within them.

We are manifestations of God's thoughts, and He has given us the same Power that He has. We have no idea how great this Power is, yet we can use it in perfect safety.

However, it is useless unless we have faith in it. When we realize that this Power has dominion over all things, and we speak from the Christ within with calm assurance, all false conditions will disappear. Our work is to cooperate with the Christ so that we may be avenues for healing in all manner of ways.

If we believe that we are powerless, we limit ourselves and the energy becomes finite. If we believe we are one with the Universe and allow ourselves to be infused with that limitless Power, the energy becomes Cosmic. We are told to acknowledge the limitless God-Power within us and then claim it as our own in every thought and activity. If we could only *feel* the reality of that Great Presence deeply, nothing could prevent us from accomplishing the same works that Jesus did.

If we know that we are One with God and let go all thoughts of sickness, we will experience Cosmic power. Then our thoughts can heal all forms of suffering, and we can heal anyone, because he or she is one with us, a Son of God as we are. Only God is expressing Himself, so there cannot be one particle of substance that is not of God; all of the Universe is one complete Whole, expressing the Divine nature of Love. Healers are told to hold this thought constantly, and to include themselves and the whole of the person seeking help as part of that Whole. If this were not so, God could not be infinite. The Truth is that God is All There Is and there is only one Life and only one Source of Life. Recognizing God as the Whole restores the essential balance between body, mind and spirit.

Several spiritual teachers imply that Cosmic Healing is perfectly safe for the healer and the one to be healed as long as the healer is unconcerned about his readiness, and about failure and success. Healers are to avoid personal involvement in the results, being just a passive instrument with pure intent and thought. Concentrating on a desire to serve God in accordance with His will, and not our own, is also necessary. However, one teacher adds the warning that there is no justification for the practice of letting the mind vacate the body and not remaining conscious of all things and people surrounding them while attempting to heal.

Causes of Disease

Nearly all the teachers make it clear that there is a mental, emotional, or spiritual cause underlying all physical pain, disease, or bodily malfunction, and that it is essential to heal the *whole* person and not just the physical symptoms. Such symptoms indicate that there is a need for change by the individual concerned; nevertheless it is common for all of us to resist and/or fear change, and such resistance or fear creates pain and blocks the healing. One teacher says that it is more important to heal the soul than the body; another that healing a disease without healing the cause merely shifts the symptoms to some other disease.

In general, the teachings state that we create all illness by our thinking, feeling, and beliefs, and that external events or symptoms are the result of internal thoughts or emotions which have created an imbalance. However, these teachings also include many references to specific mental, emotional, and spiritual causes of physical disease or pain. Most of these are fairly well known to healers, but in view of the source of this information, they are worth reviewing. They can be divided into three main categories:

Thoughts and Emotions

Fear. Anxiety. Doubt. Anger. Hate. Resentment. Bitterness. Desire for revenge. Guilt. Unresolved grief. Lust. Envy. Jealousy. Criticism. Condemnation. Stress. Abuse of the physical body. Discordant thoughts or feelings of any kind. Negative or evil thoughts. Destructive or evil activities. Taking the life of another human or desiring their death. Trying to enjoy something obtained by injustice. Saying or thinking "I am sick."

A need to learn a lesson from the illness. Overstimulation of the mind. An absence of love. A lack of spirituality in one's life. Imbalance between the physical, mental, and spiritual. Denial of God. A belief that we are separate from God and separate from other parts of God's Creation.

Past Lives

Pains or diseases originating in one or more past lives of the individual who is sick (see comments on Reincarnation later in this chapter). For example, a painful or terrifying death in a previous life may leave a memory in the soul that creates a similar pain or fear in this life. Likewise, a death from a disease or injury in a particular part of the body may leave such a strong impression in the soul's memory that in a subsequent life a weakness or vulnerability in that part of the body manifests itself.

A conflict with another individual in a previous life may have resulted in great anger, resentment, or guilt, which has been brought forward into this life, resulting in some disease or bodily malfunction until resolved by forgiveness. Usually, the other soul involved in the conflict will be reincarnated in the same time period, and the two will meet in some manner in order to provide an opportunity for such resolution.

Possession

Pain or disease caused by the possession of the sick person by a discarnate spirit entity. This cause is mentioned frequently in the New Testament and *The Aquarian Gospel* and is also referred to by the teachers in Chapters 3, 7, and 9. One teacher says that there are millions of entities on the astral plane seeking a physical vehicle that can be invaded and thus become subject to the will of the invading entity. The entity may have died of a disease and, believing it still has the disease, conveys the image and belief of that disease to the mind of the possessed individual. In other situations the very fact of two souls occupying one physical body can cause such debilitation that disease results. Sometimes the entity died as the result of an addiction to alcohol, drugs, or food, and by its craving to reexperience the sensation through being in the possessed person's body, it creates a similar addiction and illness in that person.

These last two categories add a greatly enlarged, or cosmic, dimension to the whole subject of sickness and healing. Overall, the point is made that it is very important for the sick person to learn the lesson that the illness has brought him or her.

Death

Inevitably in a study of healing we confront the fact of so-called Death—the separation of the spirit from the physical vehicle—which occurs for all of us eventually, regardless of how many times we are healed. All of the teachings have something to say about this, and they repeatedly state that there is no death, because Life is eternal. We share God's Life for eternity, because we are a part of God. Our life in a physical body, whether it is a few months or a hundred years, is but a moment in eternity. Birth is not a beginning, and death is not an ending or even a break. Nothing that God created has an end; only illusions terminate.

Life is a state of becoming, and death is a part of this process of becoming. Life involves continuous change, and birth and death are just two of the changes that we all experience. The atoms, molecules, and cells of our body are constantly dying (changing form), and being reborn. Death is but the spirit leaving the earthly body and going forth in the spiritual body; it is the Christ in us that lives forever. The difference between the physical and spiritual bodies (both of which are forms of energy) is the rate of vibration. We are warned not to cling too tightly to the earthly life; we have nothing to fear because we lose nothing that is real. Although Cosmic Power can heal all physical disease, there is a time when the physical vehicle has completed its purpose for that incarnation, and healing will not be effective.

Death cannot separate those whom love has joined. There is no separation between those who have left the physical body and those who are still in one. They are actually nearer than they have ever been. We should not grieve for them; it is selfish to do so because it retards the greater good they should be enjoying. Their joy increases when they feel that we are attuned to them in our souls, and believe and know that they are close. The veil between the worlds is very thin, and purity and faith can remove it. Communication between the two planes is always available to those who can develop, within themselves, a consciousness of the Oneness of all life.

If we let go of the physical body as a natural course of events, it will not only render transition to the spiritual level less painful, but it will become a beautiful experience. We shall find ourselves to be a living, breathing soul, more alive than ever before, for it is the soul that breathes, not the body. We shall be overwhelmed by the freedom from limitations that we shall experience. Death is the great liberator. Death does not stop the learning process of spiritual growth. The total cosmic journey of the individual soul, or higher consciousness, continues without a break.

We are also assured that the environments we shall experience after the transition are far more intense and joyful than those we have known on the earth plane. Healers need to understand that death is not a failure to heal, it is but a step on the path of life when the time is right. Jesus compares death to planting a seed in the ground, which enables it to grow and develop into a glorious tree arising from its grave.

Two of the teachers say that transplants of body parts, and other techniques that merely prolong life without curing the disease or alleviating suffering, should not be undertaken. One even says that under such circumstances the spirit may depart before physical death, so that all effort and suffering have been in vain. Another spirit teacher, whose thoughts have not been included elsewhere in this book, says that the transplanted organ and the body to which it has been transplanted become confused as to the karmic pattern they should follow, because the intended transition for both has been arrested.

One teacher says that death is an opportunity for rest and reattunement of the personal consciousness, freeing the individual from the discords of earth long enough to receive an inflow of Light and strength, which enables him or her to reexperience physical life.

Oneness and Wholeness

The concept of Oneness and Wholeness was referred to earlier, but it is so important that it is repeated and expanded upon here. There is one truth that encompasses all of the teaching and is all that is necessary for complete healing, illumination, and happiness. That is, to know and understand that *God is All There Is* and that *we are part of that Wholeness*. We are not, and cannot be, separate from God or anyone else. We are One with the Whole of Life. Here are some of the statements on this by the teachers:

There is absolutely nothing outside of God.

We are all part of God—One with Him.

If we were separate from God, He could not be infinite.

Separation is an illusion and is impossible.

The belief that we are separate from God and other beings is the cause of all disease.

Recognizing our Oneness with God and others heals with certainty.

If we identify individuals and conditions with God as the Whole, we shall demonstrate Cosmic Healing.

If we believe that we are One with the universe and allow ourselves to be infused with that limitless power, the energy becomes cosmic.

To be consciously aware of our Oneness with God is the open door to freedom.

Eventually everyone's path will lead to the same goal of Oneness.

If we could accept this truth of Oneness completely to the exclusion of all other thoughts and beliefs, we would not need anything else. If we are One, there is no one to forgive, there is no one to love or hate—we *are* Love. There is no one to heal—we are all part of God and therefore perfect. There is no one to pray to and no one to surrender to—we merely have to Be. We would not have the slightest impulse to hurt anybody or any other part of God's creation because they are all part of God, part of us—there is nothing else. Certainly we would have no fear of death—God is eternal, so death for any part of God is impossible. All concern about the past or the future would disappear—God is without beginning or end.

If this is so, then why do the teachers state that these other thoughts and activities such as love, forgiveness, changing our thinking, and so forth, are necessary? It seems that they are saying that very few people have reached the stage in spiritual development where they truly *know and understand* that we and God are all One, and until we reach that level, these other guidelines or spiritual laws are necessary if we are to grow towards that goal.

Reincarnation and Karma

All but one of the teachings include reincarnation and karma as factual. We have lived over and over again in hundreds, sometimes thousands of lives, each time in a new physical body. This gives each soul an opportunity to reestablish a balance in conditions that it has consciously thrown out of balance. There is a Law of Compensation—cause and effect—governing all the Universe. Every experience of consciousness has a former cause, and everything at the same instant is the cause of a future effect. The cause may be in a former life or in this one, in which we experience the effect.

This Law is also called Karma. When it results in a negative experience, it is not punishment—it is balance, giving us the experience we need from which to learn to avoid making the same mistake in the future. It can also be positive, giving us the peace and joy resulting from some positive action on our part in a previous life or in this one.

Karma cannot be avoided by receiving healing, nor can it be worked off vicariously. Healing can give strength of purpose and body but cannot upset the balancing effect of the illness, unless that point has already been reached. On the other hand, Jesus says that a karmic illness can be healed if the individual is willing to devote his life to one of service to humanity, and others talk of Divine Love transmuting the karma when one lives in and by the Law of Love. For example: "Disease or imbalance, caused by karma, cannot stand in the aura of Love without being transmuted."

Two of the writings (*Seth* and *Agartha*) interject the proposition that we do not live all these lives sequentially, but that they are simultaneous, because Time is an illusion and past, present, and future are all one. This is a difficult concept for most people to accept, because we deal with lineal time and sequential events every day. *A Course in Miracles* also confirms the absence of a past or a future. It further says that if the belief in reincarnation is used to strengthen the recognition of the eternal nature of Life, that is helpful, but if it is used to offer preoccupation with, or pride in, the past, or to induce inertia in the present, then it is folly.

So far the teachings have all included, and been in basic agreement on, every point that we have covered in this synthesis. However, there are a few additional subjects mentioned by only some of the writings. They are therefore mentioned here with that note of caution, although omission does not necessarily mean disagreement.

Living in the Present

One of these is the importance of living in the present, recognizing that NOW is the only time there is (chs. 1, 2 and 5). Consciousness can only create in the present. Healing can only be accomplished in the present and this releases the future. Now is Eternity and every moment of life is now. We are advised to forget the past (our own and other people's) and to let the future be taken care of by the way we live now. Seth says that "Now is the point of Power," and that this is the most important point in his teaching. We *can* change our thoughts and beliefs *now*.

Suffering

In Chapters 2, 3, 7, and 10 it is stated that suffering is inevitable for all of us on this planet. In fact, we shall eventually pass through all the stages that Jesus did, from birth to ascension; therefore everyone is crucified at one point in their spiritual journey. We are purified by our experiences and will experience the resurrection. We are told not to rebel against conditions, but rather to learn our lessons from them. Knowledge is born of suffering; awareness unfolds and suffering ceases. If our hearts are full of love, there can be no suffering.

Physical suffering is a test of faith in the power of God to heal, and healing will occur as the sufferer surrenders doubt and fear. We shall be tested and tried but always helped by the unseen forces. Once we start upon the path, much will be asked of us, but also much will be given. Nothing will be asked of us that we do not have the strength to handle. The true birth and growth of life takes place in the darkness of the earth, long before the actual blossoming in the spring. God does not inflict suffering, but He uses the suffering that man creates for himself to bring good into his life.

Silver Birch specifically talks about the necessity for healers to suffer so that they can have compassion for those seeking healing. However, it is apparent that many healers are compassionate beings and often desire to serve in this way for no other reason. It seems doubtful, therefore, that we should apply Silver Birch's observation here to all healers.

Healing by the Word

In studying these writings from higher sources another interesting clue to Cosmic Healing gradually emerged. First it was noticed that throughout *The Aquarian Gospel* there is frequent mention of "The Word." For example, after Jesus had selected his twelve disciples, he called them together to consecrate themselves to the work of God. They all prayed, and the room was shortly filled with a brilliant light, and "they heard a voice saying just one word, a word they dared not speak; it was the Sacred name of God. And Jesus said to them. . . . 'When within your souls you speak this Word, you have the keys of life and death' " (89:1–9). Later, Jesus said that man may only speak the name of God with Holy Breath, but that mercifully God had not yet revealed His name to those who could not do that (96:17–20).

"The Word" is also frequently mentioned in reports of healings performed by Jesus. For example: Mary Magdalene had been "obsessed by seven homeless spirits of the air, which had been driven out by the Omnific Word which

Jesus spoke'' (105:2). ''A man obsessed, and who was blind and dumb was brought, and Jesus spoke the Word, and lo, the evil spirits went away; the man spoke out, his eyes were opened and he saw'' (106:2). ''Jesus touched their eyes and spoke the Word. . . . they opened up their eyes and saw'' (121:35–36). Jesus sent the twelve apostles to teach and heal, and when they returned they said that ''by the sacred Word they had done many mighty works'' (123:36).

However, nowhere does the book reveal what the word was, and Jesus indicates that at that time mankind was not ready to be told. 1900 years later mankind apparently was ready, because in a series of lectures channeled through a medium before thousands (see ch. 2), Jesus told his listeners the secret of that word. He said ''The sacred Word is 'I AM.' ''* The prophets knew this eternal secret through the ages, but only a few could understand it. Later, he said that when we seem to experience disease, pain, or death, we should call the God within us into manifestation by the word of power, ''I AM.'' However, we must not speak this word unless we know the real meaning of it. When we know its meaning, we may use this word of power.

In a subsequent lecture in the same series, Jesus refers to his statement as recorded in the Bible that ''Before Abraham was, I AM'' (John 8:58) and that what he meant is that ''The spirit of the Eternal, the Christ of God, preceded all creation and that 'I AM' is the Life, not only in Abraham but in every living soul before Abraham.''

The word ''I AM'' appears in the Old Testament in one place: when God asked Moses to lead his people out of Egypt. Moses asked what he should tell the people if they

*There was an even earlier twentieth-century inspired revelation of the word in the book *Bible Mystery and Bible Meaning*, by Thomas Troward, first published in 1905. In it he concludes from an analysis of the Bible itself that the ''Lost Word'' is ''I AM.''

asked the name of the god who had told him to do this, and God replied that He was "I AM WHO I AM" (the King James version translates this as "I AM THAT I AM") and to tell them, "I AM has sent me to you" (Exodus 3:13–14). David gave a subtle hint of the Word when he quoted God as saying "Be still, and know that I am God" (Psalms 46:10).

The New Testament quotes Jesus as saying, "I am the light of the world" (John 8:12), "I am the way" (John 14:6), and "I am the resurrection and the Life" (John 11:25). Most people have interpreted these as Jesus talking about himself, but if we substitute the word *God* for "I am" in each case, a different understanding is achieved. In fact, Jesus makes it clear, in one of his shorter statements in *The I AM Discourses*, by Saint Germain, that each one of us has the same Mighty I AM Presence within us as he has. White Eagle also confirms this, stating that, "When Jesus said 'I am the light of the world' he was referring to the spark within man known throughout the spiritual world as the 'I AM,' and if we learn how to contact that 'I AM' within, we will be filled with light, health and joy."

Out of all the spirit teachings analysed for this book, the greatest emphasis on the word "I AM" is found in the writings of Saint Germain. As we have seen, the third book in that series is called "The I AM Discourses." He talks a great deal about "the Word" and clearly identified it as "I AM." He constantly talks of the God within as the individual's "Mighty I AM Presence," and that if we acknowledge, accept, understand, and feel this, its Limitless Powers will be released into our use. If we say the word "I AM" out loud, and follow it with a desired attribute, e.g. "healed," it will be manifested in the physical world. By saying the word, we are using the creative attribute of the Godhead. The vibration of the word spoken aloud releases the Power of Creation and such Divine Love, Light, Wisdom, Courage, and Activity as we cannot possibly comprehend at present.

Saint Germain cautions us not to use the word in a negative context, such as "I am sick," because it can be equally powerful in that way also.

In *Heal Thyself*, White Eagle says, "Look within yourself and find the still, ever burning white flame. Concentrate on it and you will know you are master of your life. Nothing can touch you. That Presence deep, deep within you is the I AM."

It is interesting to note that a similar belief in the enormous power of a single word has been part of the Hindu religion for thousands of years. This word is considered to be the most sacred word in the Hindu scriptures (the Vedas). It is pronounced OM or AUM, which sound is not unlike the Western "I AM." It is known as a symbol for God. Spoken out loud, it creates a vibration in mind and body which attunes the speaker with his High Self and thus with his Creator. If it is pronounced correctly, dwelling upon the final *m*, the effect is profound and has extraordinary power. The vibrations tend to attract the purer vibrations of the higher planes.

A Course in Miracles does not specifically discuss the use of this word. However, in the Workbook, which contains one lesson for every day of the year, there are statements that students are instructed to repeat frequently every day. Many of these begin with the word "I AM," thus incorporating the power of the Word without specifically mentioning this fact.

In *Agartha*, Mentor says:

> "I AM" development depends on the amount of positive energy directed toward it. . . . The opportunity for reinforcement of the "I AM" exists through everyday actions. . . . When the conscious mind releases the "I AM" to truly be, it experiences all that there is to know of the incredible nature of creation. There are no limitations on one's ability to create once in touch with the "I AM."

Conclusion

It seems clear that the basic laws of Cosmic Healing can be summarized as follows:

1. There must be unconditional love for God, for His creation, and for each living being, including oneself.

2. There must be forgiveness of all those who have hurt or angered us, as well as the asking for forgiveness of those who have been hurt by us.

3. There must be acceptance of full responsibility for our own actions, thoughts, feelings, and beliefs, as well as for the physical symptoms that manifest as a result of these.

4. To be a healer necessitates a complete surrender to God of one's own desires, ego, and will, simply wishing to serve God in any way that He directs.

5. The healing power is available to all.

6. The cause of all disease is either (*a*) abuse of our body, (*b*) various negative emotions and thoughts creating

an imbalance between mind, body, and spirit, (*c*) past lives' activity or experience needing to be balanced, or (*d*) possession by a discarnate entity.

7. Death is a rebirth, another step in the continuum that is Life. It is not a failure to heal.

8. If we know and understand that God is All There Is and that we, and all other forms of life, are part of that Wholeness, healing and illumination will follow.

9. Reincarnation and karma are part of the eternity of Life, giving us repeated opportunities to learn and grow.

10. It is important to live and heal in the present.

11. Some suffering will be experienced as we grow spiritually.

12. There is great power in the word "I AM" or "AUM." This is the name of God, and it can be used, with great reverence, in the healing process.